A Dyslexic Writes

Acknowledgements

I would never have written this book without the encouragement of Bernadette McLean, Principal of the Helen Arkell Dyslexia Centre. Bernadette is one of the UK's top brains on the subject of dyslexia but had the generosity of spirit to suggest that whilst she might be the expert on dyslexia I was the one who knew all about being a dyslexic. Her input has been invaluable.

I also wouldn't have written it without the support of my wife Fleur, who studied at Helen Arkell and now works for the Centre, and shared her learning and wisdom with me. I would also like to thank those of her friends and colleagues who made very positive noises seemingly on cue!

Normally when you write a book people try and change it a lot. Strangely the 'powers that be', as I think of those that really know what they're talking about, have been content to leave my ideas to my own devices on the basis that it's my opinion and my opinion is interesting and as valid as anybody else's. Thank you, I only hope the rest of the world treats me as kindly!

Finally I would like to thank Geoff Hayes for designing the book, and Simon dale at Forum Creative for designing and building the website.

About the Helen Arkell Dyslexia Centre

Helen Arkell was a pioneer of dyslexia and started the very first dedicated support provision in the UK. You'll find her story on the Centre's website at www.helenar-kelldyslexiacentre.com – it makes fascinating reading.

The Centre that bears her name does incredible work with and for dyslexics, both chil-dren and adults alike. Bizarrely in this politically correct world of 'education, education and education' it receives no Government of Local Authority funding – it is a charity and exists entirely on charitable donations and the money it charges for its services.

With better resources it could do even more to support a lot more dyslexic people. If after reading this (or even before) you feel inclined to support the dyslexic cause make a donation to the Centre – it will use your money extremely wisely.

Alan Campbell, September 2009

A Dyslexic Writes

An essay on dyslexia – a conundrum of conundrums

Al Campbell

Published by Helen Arkell Dyslexia Centre

Dedication

Firstly I'd like to dedicate this to my non-dyslexic wife Fleur, and my dyslexic children Phoebe and Freddie. It's been a fascinating journey so far, I can't wait to see what happens next.

Secondly I'd like to dedicate it to the parents of dyslexic children – it may be a long hard journey but the light at the end of the tunnel is most definitely on and burning brighter at every step forward. Trust me all the effort is worth it! Keep the faith and it's all onwards and upwards.

Finally this is for dyslexics everywhere, especially perhaps older dyslexics like me who never had their dyslexia assessed and acknowledged. If you're one of us rest assured the fact you might not read or write so well doesn't mean you're dim. In fact, as the evidence suggests, nothing could be farther from the truth. You're never too old to be dyslexic, but you're never too old to get something done about it.

Foreword

Alan Campbell, wordsmith and dyslexic, is possibly a conundrum himself. It may surprise many people that a dyslexic person can write so well. Al is not the first dyslexic to show his creativity in the realm of words.

This book provides us with an engaging kaleidoscope of images of one dyslexic's musings on his dyslexia. It has already proved itself enlightening for non-dyslexics to discover the elegant butterfly shifts of direction that take us, helicopter wise, from scenarios such as Hoovers, dental appointments and supervising homework. The thought of James Dyson as an honorary dyslexic is a compelling one.

Al, like many dyslexics, is unique and has a unique mind. Nevertheless, there are many recurring themes that will resonate with the dyslexic population as a whole including the well chronicled memory problems and difficulties with automaticity. Al puts real live characters on this with endearing behind closed doors glimpses of the muddles and confusions that can perplex many of the dyslexics we know and their families.

Who should read this book? I would suggest the 90% of the population who have not been granted this very much more interesting way of thinking, especially those who come in contact with these intriguing and different thinkers at home, in school/college or in the workplace.

On a personal note, I would like to state that I have learned more about dyslexia from informative conversation with its bearers than any course, conference or book I have read; educational though these other forms of learning may have been, they were not the convincer that dyslexic brains are usually much more interesting than those of us who are "otherwise abled". After more than 25 years working in this domain, I have added to my knowledge in learning about Al's brain. Bias may have helped as I have waited a long time to meet someone who could say, "You can call me Al". The Campbells were a fortunate family in that they could pay for private education when that seemed necessary for their dyslexic children.

2009 is the year we hope will be remembered when the government of this country openly acknowledged dyslexia and funded an initiative whereby every state school will have access to a specialist trained teacher.

Part of the proceeds of this book will help support dyslexics and their families until such time as that dream is realised.

Bernadette McLean

By way of an attempt at an explanation – an introduction

I like the word essay and I like being an essayist. The fact that most people consider 'an essay' to be a short piece of writing means I don't have to feel I'm writing a 'book'. More importantly for me 'to essay' is to make an attempt, to try, to be 'a trier'.

For, at the bottom of it all, this is the life of the dyslexic. We are triers. Indeed most of us have to try much harder than non-dyslexics to fulfil our potential. When we succeed we succeed well - think Sir Richard Branson, Sir Alan Sugar, Benjamin Zephaniah, Tom Cruise, Einstein, Da Vinci, Churchill, Edison, Jamie Oliver, Rick Stein and hundreds and thousands of others. Generally more men than women, although women are there too.

Before you read this book it's important you realise I have no formal qualifications to write it. My sole claims to putting fingers to keyboard and writing what follows on these pages are twofold. Firstly I am dyslexic, my son and daughter are dyslexic (more of us later). Secondly my wife (who is not in any way at all dyslexic) is a dyslexia specialist.

Equally importantly I am a writer. Being dyslexic may not be the most obvious trait for somebody who has made a reasonable go of life living by the pen. Then again as nobody told me I was dyslexic until about six years ago, when I was 50, it never really occurred to me that dyslexia might be a career limiting condition.

So this essay is a dyslexic's view of dyslexia and, as I'm expecting it to be short, say 20,000 words or so which is the sort of length most people can read in two, or three, hour-long sittings, I'm really looking forward to writing it.

It will be put together from a dyslexic's perspective, which is sometimes called in commercial business 'the helicopter view'. Dyslexics have a happy tendency to be able to see things almost from above in holistic fashion, being able to analyse a problem all at once in a 360 degree way rather than one thing at a time in a straight line.

That means it may well be 'joined-up' in a different way to how other people write stuff. One of the first things to realise about dyslexics is that we don't see things in a linear or process driven fashion. We get to the same conclusion via a different path. Hopefully you'll bear with me if ever you feel I'm losing the plot. Rest assured I'm not - after all it's my plot to begin with.

I'm writing this for all sorts of people. Firstly for those mentioned in the dedication. Secondly for all the people out there who have to live, work or care for dyslexic people. Perhaps most especially I'm writing it for parents of dyslexic children - having been a parent of two dyslexics myself I have first-hand knowledge of both the worries parents endure, and the frustrations and lack of self-esteem the children suffer.

If you fall into this parenting category let me say right up-front that dyslexia need not be a long term problem. For sure the early years can be tough but, because by definition dyslexic kids are generally pretty bright, we all tend to live happily ever after. You need to spot the dyslexia early, and get the right support (and most likely pay for most of it), but both my son and daughter ended up being straight A students and also played sport at junior international level. From my perspective being the parent of a dyslexic child has been the most rewarding thing in the world.

Finally of course I'm writing this for myself - if I've learned one thing about dyslexics (and myself) over the years it's that we have enormous curiosity about how things work, or don't, and why. So, this is my attempt to join up and explain my own dyslexic brain to myself.

The world of dyslexics and dyslexia is a world of conundrums. As my wife rightly points out the first conundrum in this book of conundrums is the fact that very few dyslexics (hopefully aside from dyslexic parents) will probably ever bother to read it. Most dyslexics don't take much to reading the written word. Perhaps that's why I've kept the world fooled for so long.

The essential health warning

We live in an age where everything comes with a health warning - this essay is no exception. I, Al Campbell, have written this essay, which makes me its author. However it's important to understand that just because I am an author of an essay on dyslexia it doesn't mean I'm an authority on dyslexia. All it really means is that I'm opinionated, passionate enough to commit those opinions to paper, and hopeful that people might not only be interested enough to read them but be prepared to pay to do so. If you paid, thank you.

You must also consider that my background as a marketing man means my opinions are rather generic. Marketeers tend to take a 'most of the people, most of the time' approach. That means our opinions can be somewhat broad. This essay is not a 'study' of dyslexia or dyslexics, more of a general overview based on personal observations.

Naturally before I publish I will have the content sanity checked by those with much more detailed expertise. Hopefully we won't dicker too much over the detail. However I know there will be small points I've left out as not being relevant to my stream of thought. On a 'most of the people, most of the time' basis my thoughts will also not extend to those with greater challenges such as dyspraxia, aspergers syndrome, ADHD etc. I have no knowledge of those.

Therefore the health advice is take my opinions as opinions and not as wisdom, and treat them with all due care and attention. After all some people don't even believe such a thing as dyslexia exists.

However if reading this makes you think you, or someone you know, might be facing dyslexic challenges, good advice would be to go and find somebody who can give you an authoritative and definitive opinion and help you find ways around any problems that might exist.

Dyslexia - the executive overview

If you fall into the category of those who believe dyslexia might exist you might like me to be up-front about some defining points to help you get your head around what comes next and later. In marketing we would call this the 'Executive Overview' - a bit you put at the front of a longer report to give the person who commissioned it the heads-up of the overall situation. Generally he or she will be too busy or too important to read the rest and important folk never really 'do detail'.

Experts argue but in general terms it seems probable that somewhere between 1 in 10 and 1 in 8 people have some form of dyslexic challenge. At one level 1 in 10 doesn't sound that many. Get offered a 10% discount in the High Street these days and you probably wouldn't bother to walk across the road for it. At another level if you got a 10% pay rise on your salary, or could get 10% more marks in an exam, you'd probably think it was well worth having.

Anyway on the basis that your average double-decker bus takes around 70 people, come rush hour there will be 7 or 8 dyslexic people on every bus you see. With the UK population standing somewhere around 60 million that means the population of dyslexics is somewhere between 6 and 7.5 million. That's a lot of people, and most of us will know more than a few of them. As adults you work with us, play with us and drink down the pub with us, and there's every chance you don't realise we are any different.

Actually by the time we dyslexics get to be adults the differences are often not that apparent. At the 'heads-up' level the difference can be explained quite simply - somewhere between an egg being fertilised and a baby popping out Mother Nature decided to experiment with the established blueprint she drew up for the other 90% of human kind and bugger about with the wiring diagram in our brains.

Being clever she knew she was making life more difficult to start with, so in the majority of cases she gave us more brain power to be able to compensate. By the time we get to adulthood the vast majority of us have worked out how to appear normal down the pub or in the office and many of us have used our differently equipped minds to be poets or scientists or inventors or entrepreneurs.

In strategic terms this can be seen as a very sound diversification tactic by Mother Nature. Keeping 90% of your human capital ring-fenced by 'normality' whilst speculating with the other 10% represents the sort of prudent investment strategy the world's banks would have been wise to follow during 2008. You end up with an evolutionary strategy whereby the 10% act as a benchmark against which the behaviour of the other 90% can be challenged and potentially improved.

When Einstein, who was not only famous but famously dyslexic, died he left his brain to science. When doctors came to look at it they were amazed. By all accounts he had the most uniquely wired-up brain ever seen.

You might already start to see a pattern emerging here - there are not that many dyslexic doctors, but any number of dyslexic scientists. Doctors function best when every 'body' works in the same manner. Having to account for things they don't expect causes stress. I'll only whisperingly suggest it at this stage, but one thing you might conclude before you get to the end of my ponderings is that teachers come out of the same mould.

Dyslexia - the conundrums of conundrums

Conundrum is a nice sounding word and I enjoy saying it and using it a lot. I should probably look up the dictionary definition, but then again, as you're not likely to, I hope we'll be on the same page if I say that for me a conundrum is a problem or situation that's hard to understand and explain. Quite simply we see something we don't expect and we can't easily account for it.

And there, in a nutshell, you have dyslexia.

Actually I should say that 'there in a series of nutshells' you have dyslexia. Experts are coming round to the view that there is a whole range of 'dyslexias' that show up differently in different people. That to me makes a lot of sense - certainly when I look at the dyslexic people I know it looks like a whole heap of conundrums strung together, and rarely all the same ones or in the same order.

The communication and understanding conundrum

I may not be an authority on dyslexia but I can reasonably claim to be an authority on effective communication. As a copywriter and messaging strategist I've spent most of my working life helping people communicate better to help large groups of people understand more things more clearly more easily.

After all those years I have discovered the ultimate truth about communication, which I'll happily share with you now: communication only occurs at the point when the message being communicated has been understood.

Whilst this may be something of a no-brainer, in my experience most people think communication occurs at the point the message was delivered. We're all guilty. As parents, because we've told our kids something, we think it's been communicated. Then we're amazed when they do the opposite. The same is true of many teachers - they give the lesson/seminar/tutorial and think 'that's that done, they know that now'.

I found this postcard in a tourist shop the other day that isn't about this sort of dyslexic mis-communication but which sums it up pretty well for me. It reads:

'I know you believe you understand what you think I said, but I'm not sure you realise that what you heard is not what I meant'

In business I've sat in any number of presentations and, when I've asked people what they thought about it, had feedback along the lines of 'that guy had terrible taste in ties'. The message here is that if all people remember about your presentation is the colour of your tie all you have communicated to the audience is the colour of your tie.

If you ever have any responsibility at all for delivering communication this needs careful thinking about. In the first place are you expecting too much by communicating too much? Personally I try never to put more than 3 bullet points on a presentation slide - might get up to 5 if it all joins up concisely, but after that I'll split the slides.

Listen to the great politicians and they tend to work in threes too. Tony Blair used to work out the three points he wanted to get across and say them over and again. Better still he'd say them in alternative words - he knew different people take things in different ways and that frequency and repetition count heavily in communication.

In large parts this takes us beyond simple communication and 'message take out' and into the realms of memory and retention - of which much more later.

If you want an alternative view on this, human resources people tend to have a refreshingly different approach. A line manager trying to communicate with his staff will say 'I told him that, he got it wrong, why didn't he understand? An HR/training professional will say 'he didn't understand that, what did I get wrong, how should I have told him?'

On the basis that the majority of the time we communicate as human beings we're trying to share ideas and persuade people to learn something or perform in a certain way, it's worth considering who owns the responsibility for communication being effective. Is it the person delivering or the person receiving it? Just because some of us don't understand something first time round it doesn't mean we're stupid! Tell us again, tell us differently and check our body language until you're sure we've understood.

Understanding 'understanding' - the learning conundrum
If you're the sort of person who is prepared to accept ownership of a communication process it seems only reasonable you need to develop a good understanding of how the people you're communicating with/to 'understand' and learn things. Essentially experts agree there are three predominant styles of learning and therefore three different types of 'learners':

Visual learners: these are the people who prefer to get things into their brains by taking in the information through their eyes. They love reading stuff and are in heaven when information is given to them in writing on blackboards/whiteboards. About 30% of the population prefer to learn visually.

Audio learners: these are the people that process information best when they take it in through their ears. They like to be told stuff. Wrap it all up in a story context and they'll love you for ever. Around 35% of people tick this box.

Kinaesthetic learners: discovering there is such a thing as a kinaesthetic learner immediately made me realise why I held the record as the most corporally punished boy at primary school due to the fact I was such a fidget, couldn't sit still and kept fiddling with my pencils/rubber/the inkwell and sundry accoutrements and learning type paraphernalia. I was also a great doodler. Nobody seems quite sure how we learn best - it's a sort of osmosis thing. We account for whatever percentage is left.

Actually few people are 100% one thing or another and most people have a combination of learning styles. It's well established that when you communicate using a combination of audio and visual media most of the people most of the time take out and remember much more.

Observationally though dyslexics mostly seem to lean heavily towards the kinaesthetic category. We not only fiddle with stuff, we look out of the window, avoid eye contact, and hate being made to sit still and told to 'concentrate' - bizarrely we can only concentrate when we're not sitting still. We're often quite vocal and whilst we're happy to speak up we don't like putting things down on paper - generally because we can't!

The teaching conundrum

By understanding the understanding conundrum we set up the major challenge for dyslexics faced with a classroom environment. Whilst most dyslexics are mostly kinaesthetic, the majority of teachers are mostly visual. So at the front of the class we have this person who wants to write things on a board expecting everybody to sit still and follow. Meanwhile we're fidgeting away wanting to say stuff.

No wonder dyslexics can often be called 'disruptive' - from the teacher's perspective we must look like nightmare problem children. At the same time it can seem that we're not learning and performing, and there is genuinely every chance we're not. And unless we're spotted early the older we get the less well we perform.

Another conundrum here is whether teachers are the best people to be teachers. They come from the smallest category of learners - for every 3 visual learners there are 7 who are not. This conundrum self-perpetuates because visual learners are very good at following processes and writing things down, and people who have qualified as teachers pick the next generation of trainees, and the most visual of all are those who tend to set curriculums and have obsessions with exams and measuring performance. Do you see a pattern emerging here?

Of course I'm doing the teaching profession at large a disservice and being over-critical. In many respects teachers only deliver or administer what 'educationalists' (generally senior 'old-school' style teachers elevated to policy making) benchmark as expected performance. With regard to dyslexia the green shoots of enlightenment seem to be thrusting onwards and upwards. We dyslexics just have to hope they are nurtured to fruition.

The teaching/learning/education/training/coaching conundrum
Has it ever occurred to you that we train teachers but teach children? In the lexicon of dyslexia this should strike anyone as a conundrum. Why do we use two different words? Are teaching and training two different processes and, if they are, should they be? And if training is what teachers need don't children need it too?

As ever in life there are more questions than answers.

For example what about educators? 'Educators' seem to be those responsible for aggregate learning, whereas teachers own delivery of specific parts. As teachers get more experience the career path leads towards management and they become educators and set the expectations of performance.

Training seems to reside within the area of establishing 'practice'. In the lexicon of dyslexia 'practice' is a significant word, and seems to be used in several different ways. When you talk about 'Best Practice' you're discussing the concept of delivery. When you say to a dyslexic child 'best practise!' you're giving jolly good advice about learning and study skills. Dyslexia experts call this sort of same sound but different spelling and different meaning a 'homophone'.

The performance conundrum

Mankind is a competitive species and highly focused (obsessed even?) on performance. It seems to have become increasingly important to know where any individual, team or slice of population is positioned in terms of performance against every other. We take security in performing well, and in being 'good' at stuff. Being good at stuff opens doors that let us go on and do more stuff or at least the next stuff.

Make no mistake we dyslexics are every bit as competitive as the rest of you and possibly more so. Life makes us driven to succeed and we'll be out there punching above our weight long after many others have gone home.

Performance is linked to success. Success is linked to money, status, and probably fundamentally the ability to attract a range of sexual partners. Whoever said success breeds success was pretty astute - and may have been pretty into the bargain.

Performance, or the lack of it, is fundamental to dyslexia and even more fundamental in its assessment. In itself performance isn't the conundrum, it's the expectation of performance - which is so tightly focused on age-based benchmarks. Educationalists want everybody to progress at a regular and predictable rate and make their plans and policies accordingly - at least in the UK.

I have nephews in France who didn't meet the expectation and were simply asked to re-do a year. This can also happen in the private sector - if you're paying for your education privately the school doesn't mind going over the ground again. It's good business and by the time you're 25 nobody gives a tinkers that you took exams later than your peers.

The fact is the real world doesn't mind whether you pass your GCSEs and A levels when you're 15 or 25. Or whether you pass them or get the grades you want at first time of asking. Or whether you pass 10 in a sitting or take two every year for five years.

The expectation conundrum

At the bottom of it all the question for both parents and educators alike has to revolve around the question of whether the 10% of the world that is dyslexic should expect (and be expected) to fit in with 90% that isn't, and/or vice versa.

The establishment jury may be out on that one for some time. My wife and I chose to take the jury out of the equation and sent both our kids down the independent route. It probably wouldn't have mattered so much with our daughter Phoebe who may well have thrived in the right sort of state school. For our son Freddie however we felt there was no real option.

All my experience suggests that the more dyslexic you are the more you need all the support you can get/afford as soon as you can afford it. So the real problem facing parents is 'how dyslexic is he/she?' And that's all about assessment.

The parental conundrum - part 1

When we moved our kids to the independent sector we were fortunate enough to have the money. Nothing lasts forever and at the end of the day, as fortunes changed, we ended up selling the house to cover school fees. Many of my friends thought we were daft - especially when times got tougher. In the first instance we were lucky in being able to afford it, then perhaps we were unlucky in being locked into it.

Most parents don't have the option of affording independent or even extra tuition, and the policy here needs to be reviewed. A few (and fewer these days) have the resources to not even have to think twice about paying. In between there are parents who can afford to pay for some element of education. The question is which bit do you buy and when?

My personal advice would be that the moment you start to suspect your child may be dyslexic find the money for a professional assessment. If the assessment suggests dyslexia the state system will start to take notice and you can expect some professional support - you'll get this too in the independent sector but they may charge extra for it.

Normally dyslexia starts to manifest around the age of 7 - because you're looking at things like spelling and reading and writing it's quite hard to test for it before this. If you catch it this early you can make a decent strategic plan for education. You can also support your child at home. With early support the years your child is most at risk from the negative aspects of dyslexia will be when they change school. If you've got money, that's probably the best time to spend it.

Once again assessment is the key.

The assessment conundrum

Dislocate your finger and you can put it back in place and have it working properly within days. Cut it off and you can have it stitched back on with no major detriment - I know this for a fact as our son Freddie crushed his finger in a swing door at London Zoo when he was two and had it sewn back together by the Neurosurgery team at University College Hospital. They were absolute stars, the finger is perfect.

The great thing about fingers is that the problem is in plain view, the symptoms are obvious and the cause of the problem doesn't matter. You simply treat what you see and everything gets better.

Dislocate certain brain functions and it all becomes a bit of a mystery. The only way you can really assess dyslexia is to look for what's not there that you think should be. We knew Fred had 'challenges' when he first went to primary school, he was suspected as dyslexic by several teachers and was having special support by the age of 9, but wasn't 'formally diagnosed' as dyslexic until he was assessed by an educational psychologist when he was almost 12.

Since then he's been helped by another load of absolute stars, and received appropriate concessions come exam time. The fact is that when it comes to assessing dyslexia there are always some areas of doubt, the 'system' takes some time to kick-in to action, and there is no quick fix. You wouldn't know Freddie ever trashed his finger, and there isn't even a scar. Conversely he'll be dyslexic for the rest of his life, on top of which he'll always carry some 'mental scars' from his early years of schooling, as will we as his parents.

Let's not beat about the bush we 10% of the world who are dyslexic are abnormal. If our patterns of behaviour and performance were normal there wouldn't be a problem. Or there might be, but it would be the other people who had it. As a group we should be thankful that the behaviour and performance of the other 90% is so predictable.

The abnormality conundrum

I'm adding this bit in as an aside after my wife visibly cringed at my use of the word 'abnormal' in the above paragraph. Abnormal isn't the sort of word they use much in education. In educationalist terms we are people with 'special needs' - a term which quite frankly I find patronising. Only Jose Mourinho is 'the special one' and we all know what most of the world thinks of him!

We don't have special needs, just different ones. People on 'special diets' need them because if they eat a 'normal' diet it can give them health problems and could even kill them. We don't need to learn anything different from normal people, we need exactly the same diet of information and knowledge sharing. We just need it served up in a different way. Perhaps we're the 10% that need hot chilli in our learning to give it a bit of a kick. Or, more likely, a Masterchef in the kitchen. Although rather a lot of chefs are one of us.

So, I'm fine with the term abnormal because that's how I feel happiest seeing myself - really quite significantly different from the rest and actually proud of it. However if the term offends your sensitivities please feel free to substitute non-normal in its place.

Defining what is abnormal is where performance, allied to years of scientific statistical observation of children learning stuff becomes an essential measure. Take the concept of 'reading-age'. The expectation of reading-age is completely performance based. All you need to do is take a thousand 9.4 year olds (although purely in statistical terms a sample of 200 would do), work out what most of them can read comfortably most of the time, and you've got a factual benchmark.

Use that reading material as a test piece for others and you can judge if someone the same age is within their comfort zone. If they have problems reading the piece it is reasonable to assume there is some 'disconnect' with what's normal. Similarly there's a disconnect if they can read a piece meant for children of 12.6 - although this is not normally cause for concern.

In ways like this a dyslexia assessment is a rather sophisticated 'health check' of an individual's ability to perform against a statistically proven expectation and, with younger people at least, can give a quick and fairly accurate result. The tests involve numbers, shapes, comprehension, reading real words, reading 'non-words' (made up ones that don't exist but test the ability to translate letters into recognisable sounds), word association, spatial awareness and more.

Part of the assessment may be an IQ test. As a general rule the final judgement may be made based on determining IQ and then using that as a benchmark, along with age, to assess test performance. Over time thousands of people all around the world have taken IQ tests and other tests and a profile of expected performance has been standardised.

The IQ conundrum

The fact that IQ is a 'quotient' of 'intelligence' defines the fact that it is positioning any individual within a range of performances that have been recorded and analysed from a large population. In practice any individual may perform slightly better or slightly worse on a different day, but by and large the first time you do a formal IQ assessment you've got a benchmark of your own intelligence relative to the world at large.

That doesn't mean everybody with the same IQ will answer all the same questions the same way. But overall they should have the same engine power.

IQ, like dyslexia, is something we're born with and doesn't go away. We may not perform as well or as quickly at some tasks as we get older, but that's an age thing. Some experts suggest you can improve your IQ, but in real terms any degree of change is small. On this basis IQ isn't a conundrum at all, it's more like your height when fully grown, or being left-handed - it's a given.

To give an easily readable measure of comparison the 'average' IQ is given as 100. Score more than 100 and you're more intelligent than average. Score less, and it's the other way around. However the very nature of any population means there will be more people nearer to average than further away from it. Therefore there are lots of people with an IQ of say 105 or 95, but very few at 130 or 70. The higher or lower you go the smaller the population gets.

Interpretation of Evaluation Results

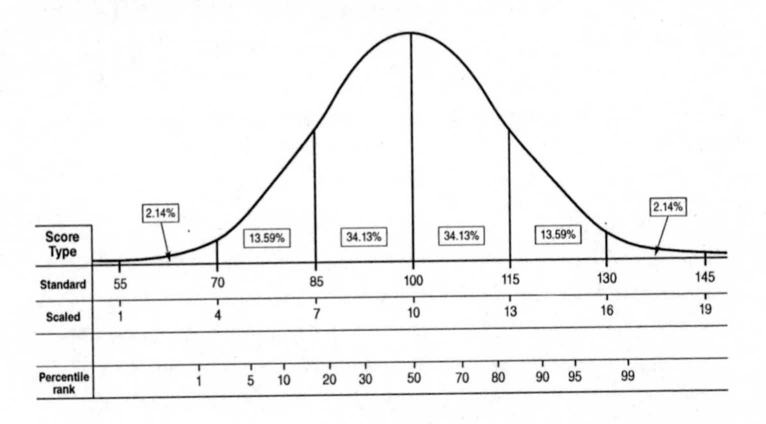

If you record the IQ of any large population you get what science refers to as a 'bell-shaped' graph or 'standard distribution'. To make IQ more meaningful in terms of assessment the IQ graph is turned into 'centiles' (or percentiles) which represents what proportion of a population will have that IQ. As you might expect an average IQ of 100 puts you on the 50th centile, bang in the middle. Sit in a football stadium of 50,000 people and 25,000 of those around you will be more intelligent and 24,999 will be less intelligent - or thereabouts.

As you move away from the middle things start to change. For example an IQ of 130 puts you round about the 96th centile. In that same stadium a person on the 96th centile could expect only 200 people to be more intelligent and 48,799 people to be less intelligent. So whilst in IQ terms you're only 30 points above average you're actually 46% above average (which could sound like being almost twice as bright). So, perhaps there is a conundrum after all.

Back in the day there used to be something called the 11 plus, which was an IQ test - these days it would be called a non-verbal reasoning test. If memory serves an IQ of 112 or above meant they sent you to grammar school. Back in that same day they reckoned that you needed an IQ of 120 or more to get to University - it wouldn't be anywhere near that high today.

The statistical conundrum

To me there is a major disconnect in the way some of these things are measured and reported, especially in the way education considers 'averages'.

IQ is measured on a sliding scale where 100 is the middle, or more properly 'median', figure. The 'median' is the number that will occur most frequently in any sample. In IQ more people will have an IQ of 100 than any other figure.

The median crops up once again in aged-based performance. If you are 10.6 and have a reading age of 10.6 you are de facto the median in a group of 10.6 year olds. In effect you are exactly average.

However in IQ terms educationalists consider there is an 'average range' which runs between a standardised IQ score of 85 and 115. Turn this into a 'centile' score and it becomes nonsense - at the bottom end you are on the 15th centile and at the top end on the 85th centile. In a random cohort of 1000 people somebody on the 85th centile would only have 150 people 'brighter' than they are. At the bottom end, on the 15th centile, you would have 850 people 'brighter' than you.

Assessors, when reporting, talk about 'low average' and 'high average'. I think this simply fudges the issue, especially when the aged-based performances are based on a median figure which is right in the middle of the bell shaped curve. The fact is that educationalists consider that anybody who falls within this 'average range band' does not really need any specific educational provision.

The real problem as far as the real world is concerned is that the 'average' band covers around 68% of the population, which is either a complete nonsense or a truly bizarre mathematical spin on the true facts. This might be realistic if it was a range of the middle 20%, but from the layman's point of view it is a little bit of political correctness gone mad.

Meanwhile, back at the assessment conundrum...

As a benchmark you can assess the level of performance of a whole group of people with any given IQ. Having done so it stands to reason that any other person with the same IQ should have the potential to perform similar tasks to a similar level. Armed with that knowledge you can assess any other individual to see if they do indeed perform to a scientifically and statistically proven expectation.

If your IQ puts you on the 85th centile and your performance in a specific task (say remembering a sequence of numbers) suggests you are on the 15th centile, there is a disconnect. It's not what you'd expect. In diagnostic terms something is missing.

So, now nearly 5,000 words into this essay we can come up with what seems to me to be the most reasonable definition of dyslexia:

Dyslexia is something that prevents an individual from performing tasks to the levels you would normally expect given his or her true potential.

And the tasks concerned may be anything from reading and writing, to remembering to put the cat out for the night.

The normality conundrum

'Normality' is the key comparison for determining dyslexia. As mentioned above we dyslexics shouldn't beat about the bush, we should accept we're abnormal. Then again you could say, whether dyslexic or not, David Beckham has an abnormal ability to convert free kicks into goals, or that Dawn French has an abnormal facility to make us laugh. It's not a bad thing at all - one person's abnormality may well turn out to be somebody else's talent.

So the BIG question is 'what's normal'. A friend of mine had a Yorkshire Grandmother whose favourite saying was 'all the world's a little bit queer save thee and me, and even thee's a little strange sometimes'. That of course was back in the day when it was normal to say 'queer' with no risk of being politically incorrect. Which just goes to illustrate that normality, or the perception of what's normal (or acceptable as normal), can be a moveable feast.

In terms of large populations 'what's normal' perhaps brings us back to my marketing adage of how most of the people behave most of the time. However that doesn't account for populations that may be smaller, but which are still substantial.

For example if you 'Google' left-handedness you'll discover that the commonly held belief is that about 1 in 10 people are left handed (see where I'm going here?). In fact recent research amongst 3,000 schoolchildren in Waltham Forest (shouldn't they have been in school?) suggests that figure is wrong and that in fact 11.6% of boys are left-handed, whilst only 8.6% of girls is left handed. There are suggestions that the figure is rising due to greater social acceptance.

Wikipedia goes for the 10% figure or even less in America. I find that strange as every time I go to America I really notice how many 'lefties' there are. Then again Wikipedia will probably be written by a team of predominantly right-handed people. Whilst surfing I also learn that Barack Obama is left-handed, and that there is only one gay left-handed Jewish Congressman. Don't you just love the internet?

So, by definition left-handedness is abnormal, and given the Latin word for left-handed is 'sinister' it has been viewed as suspicious. Conversely 'dexter', which gives us admirable words like 'dexterity' and 'dextrous' is Latin for right-handed. The question is does being left-handed in a right-handed world cause you problems?

As a dextrous boy myself this question never occurred to me. I naturally assumed God had made some people that way so they could play on the left wing in the football team. I spent hours training myself to kick a football against a garage door with my left foot, as my school team had a vacancy at left-half and I wasn't good enough at the time to play anywhere else.

At Grammar school, where we had to start using ink pens, it started to become apparent that lefties had problems. In my year the lefties either had dreadful writing or scribed beautifully with an italic nib. Left-handedness finally became a personal problem for me at University when I used to crash in a flat with a leftie who had been sent a left-handed cork screw by an Uncle in America. Ever tried opening a bottle of wine right-handed with a left-handed cork screw? Even worse if you've just come back from the pub.

The final illustration was my one visit to Saville Row to order a bespoke suit. 'Is Sir right-handed or left handed?' the tailor enquired. I asked him why this mattered. 'Most left-handed gentlemen prefer a left-handed fly sir,' came the reply, 'they find it makes the little things in life easier.' One does not want to be too graphic in the development of this particular argument, but it is certainly one area where left handed males are at a disadvantage if they buy their suits in M&S.

On the plus side Jimi Hendrix was a leftie, played a right handed guitar upside down and changed the rock genre forever. To my knowledge nobody has ever suggested Jimi was dyslexic but read between the lines, factor in his completely different take on the way a guitar should be played, and you wouldn't be getting very good odds down at Joe Corals on the fact he was anything but one of the chosen 10%.

All things considered as a man I'd rather be dyslexic than a leftie in a world of right-handed fly buttons. Without labouring the point there is a whole population of people out there for whom being left-handed is absolutely normal, even though it means they have to learn strategies to cope with a dextrous world the same way a man with a dodgy knee learns to walk with a limp.

However whilst lefties have been sensibly integrated into society, and have web sites and products devoted to their singularities that allow them pride in their individuality, the population of dyslexics still need to discover a sense of identity around which they can bond and feel secure.

The children's peer group conundrum.
Left-handedness is now an established and accepted 'abnormality'. Hey, in America, anybody left-handed can claim he or she is just like the President, and nobody messes with the Commander-in-Chief. Dyslexia has yet to reach that level of acceptance and nowhere is this more clearly demonstrated than among children.

Civilisation has led most of us adults most of the time to accommodate and accept differences within our fellow humans. We are less racist, less homophobic, less judgemental and generally more tolerant of people who are not entirely like us.

But we were not born that way. We learn to be civilised as we grow up. We learn tolerance and kindness. However as children we are still suspicious and critical of those who 'don't fit in'. The 90% don't understand or tolerate the 10%. By herd instinct they marginalise us - dyslexics have to not only work harder academically, but socially too. Often we are bullied - more about this later if my dyslexic memory doesn't fail me.

The genetic conundrum

There are studies that suggests that for every one dyslexic girl born there will be somewhere between 4 and 8 dyslexic boys (it depends which reference you take). Others suggest it's a 3:2 ratio. Apparently it's probably something to do with the X chromosome. There appears to be no rational explanation for this, although girls tend to be undiagnosed for longer. Whatever, if you are a dyslexic male there is a good chance you will pass on what is popularly called the 'dyslexia gene'.

The knowledge versus skill set conundrum

A small point but perhaps a big question: 'what is knowledge, and how is it linked to performance?' My best guess is that knowledge is everything we understand about the world that isn't instinct and that it's linked to performance in as much that you can't do something if you don't know how.

Knowledge is personal to everybody. We're not born with knowledge, so we have to acquire it. Knowledge is the sum of all the things we've learned on our journey through life. Typically the longer the journey the greater the knowledge.

However performance is much more linked to skill sets, although skill sets are also learned. Being tested on your knowledge generally revolves around having to write things down. It may also require the ability to read a question in the first place.

In my view, the ability to read and write falls firmly into the 'skills' category. There are any number of people who possess great skills of reading and writing who, when tested, don't have much 'knowledge' to put on paper. Then again there are any number of people who have great knowledge without the skill set to write it down in any coherent or articulate fashion. Who should we value most highly?

The intellectual conundrum

Knowledge starts off being fact based - a piece of learning that can be regurgitated in response to a question from the framework within which it was acquired. What's 2 x 2? Four. What's the capital of France? Paris. That sort of thing.

The ability to draw upon and combine various chunks of knowledge and then work out something that adds to your knowledge without being taught requires intellectual ability. We're talking about Newton watching an apple fall to the ground and coming up with the concept of gravity. Nobody taught him that a greater mass will draw a smaller mass towards it - Newton invented it, or at least he described and defined it.

In many respects intellectual ability is more highly valued than knowledge or skill. Einstein's insight that E=MC2 gave us perhaps the most famous equation in the world. In practical terms of course it has no great day-to-day use whatsoever unless you want to make an atomic bomb.

However the ability to solve problems is important - finding the right answer is always good. More important still is the ability to work out what the question or problem is in the first place. Einstein was famously dyslexic, as are many other 'inventors' and discoverers. The dyslexic gene is a very inquisitive one. When we used to get a new pitch brief at the advertising agency we used to have a meeting that started off 'what's the exam question?' Strangely people with a problem they want you to solve rarely know what the real problem is.

The mother of inventors conundrum

Necessity may be the mother of invention but I would strongly argue that dyslexia is the mother of inventors. Dyslexics see problems and solutions in a different light. We look at things in a way that others do not. Society at large needs dyslexics to challenge the perceived wisdom and challenge the status quo.

I have no idea if James Dyson is dyslexic but if he isn't we should make him an honorary one today. Here is a man with a passion for a different sort of vacuum cleaner. In a land ruled by King Hoover, James Dyson saw a different way of doing it and didn't give up until the world stood up and took notice. In actual fact the world might not have needed a different sort of vacuum cleaner. The point is that there is more than one solution to any problem.

Science and invention is a safe haven for dyslexics. It's a place where things are written down in very simple symbolic codes of letters, symbols or numbers. Scientists communicate with other scientists incredibly quickly and efficiently. If you're a non-scientist equations may all look like gobbledegook. If so, welcome to the flipside of dyslexia - that's exactly what a lot of dyslexics feel about traditional written language.

The point is you can either write 'energy is equal to mass multiplied by the speed of light squared' or you can write $E=MC^2$. It's simply two different ways of saying the same thing and the latter is much more efficient provided you 'know the code'.

The code conundrum

Written language is a code, spoken language is a code and body language is a code. Hey, no wonder it's tough to learn stuff, especially when you can write something down, speak the words in a way that puts different emphasis on the original meaning, and then do things with your body shape or arms or face that conflicts with both. And we haven't even started to talk about the fact that words spelled the same can have different meanings as can words that are spoken the same.

Before you can possibly begin to join-up anything in life you have to break the code in which the information is delivered. If you can't do that, or have trouble doing it, or if your brain wants to decodify stuff in a different way, you're going to struggle a bit to understand stuff at the start. You'll also need to unravel another code called 'context'. The words 'hare' and 'hair' both sound pretty much the same but would be used in very different circumstances.

One of the problems with the English language is that its code is pretty random and unorthodox. Its randomness centres around the fact that different bits of the code (the letters) sound different in different contexts and juxtapositions with other bits of the code. Learning to break the code is essentially about joining-up several senses at once - you use your eyes to translate something into a sound that you then quality control check using your ears while at the same time seeking contextual clues that add value to the meaning.

The phonics conundrum

One of the things at the heart of most dyslexic problems is phonics - the way we translate letter shapes into sounds, and equally importantly vice versa. Humans have been merrily talking away to each other for thousands of years. As far as most of the people most of the time are concerned we've been writing down the words we use to communicate for less than two centuries.

The brain may be a very sophisticated thing, and it needs to be. It has to turn letter shapes into sounds, and sounds into letter shapes. In reading out loud vision drives speech - your eyes need to drive your lips and your tongue and your breathing. If you're writing something down that's being spoken, your ears need to drive your hands. Worst of all when you do an exam you have to remember echoes of what you've seen and heard rattling round inside your head and use your hands to communicate quite complex issues in total silence.

The teaching of phonics, or not as the case may be, and the fashions in how phonics have or have not been taught, has been a contentious issue for the last four decades. Should we be surprised? I think not!

The automaticity conundrum

So, life is tough enough out there at the far reaches of the learning curve even if you're part of the 90% normality. If you're part of the 10% it can be a couple of degrees tougher.

Because the security of humanity has become based upon a common acceptance of civilisation, we need to live by convention. Every mature human being has the right to expect to live in a mature culture and society where everybody behaves according to the same rules. Most importantly not only do we expect people to all behave in the same certain way, we expect them to do it automatically.

Now automaticity is a strange word. You don't much hear it outside education or the science of robotics - it is the expectation that somebody will respond like an 'automaton', that is in 'a machine like way that is consistently repetitive in response' to a given stimulus.

Strange word or not understanding the concept of automaticity is central to all the many and varied conundrums that surround dyslexia and dyslexics. In a concise and jargonistic way to call dyslexia a 'dysfunction in the conventional automaticity of knowledge' might be just about as straightforward a definition as you can get. Assuming of course you know what the words mean.

The fact is that whilst dyslexics may be great at solving problems most of life is not problematic. We learn stuff when we are young in order to manage out life's problems in the first place. Humans function most successfully at life when they can access most of the knowledge they need most of the time instantly.

When was the battle of Hastings? 1066! What's seven times four? Twenty eight! How many minutes in an hour? Sixty! How many letters in the alphabet? Twenty six! What's the capital of America? Washington!

All these questions and hundreds of others are about stuff we can answer by regurgitating a nugget of knowledge automatically. The bizarre thing is that as facts they are all of very little practical use. Your life won't depend upon knowing this sort of stuff and your job probably won't either.

Education is obsessed with facts - is it more important to know where Newcastle is rather than tell you how to apply for a mortgage on a house there? Which bit of that don't they teach you at school? It's much more useful to know how to make a cup of tea than the fact that water boils at 100 centigrade. Anyway knowledge goes out of fashion (or convention) - back in the day water used to boil at 212 Fahrenheit but now you can't mention it.

Realistically you wouldn't expect anybody to automatically know the answer to 74 x 47 - it's not a question that comes up very often, if at all, in the humdrum of daily existence. However it wouldn't be unreasonable to expect most people to know the process or convention for working it out (even if that process is punching buttons on a calculator) and that, given time, a correct answer could be delivered.

So in the simple areas of life automaticity is about an instant knowledge based answer. As things get more complicated it's about being able to instantly access a method of working out the answer. In many instances it is a case of the instantly accessed knowledge nugget being a building block for a more complicated answer - if you don't know what 2 x 2 is you won't be able to work out 22,222 x 2.

Automaticity in behaviour is equally important. We look before we cross the road. We drive on the left (well in the UK anyway). We don't stir up hornets' nests. To forget these automatic responses can be a life limiting strategy.

On another level Venus Williams doesn't have to think about hitting a forehand passing shot - she probably doesn't have time to think about it. Wayne Rooney scores goals seemingly by instinct. In his heyday Tiger Woods put his drive on the fairway with monotonous regularity. The fact Meryl Streep knows her lines inside out means she can concentrate on the acting. Automaticity is good, we value it very highly.

Put all these things into context and you come to one simple conclusion - life is a memory test. The better and faster you can remember things, the more successful you are likely to be.

The memory conundrum

Wouldn't life be simple if we could remember everything we were told for ever? Just like the people on Eggheads we would be mines of information. Very handy if you want to win Who Wants to be a Millionaire? But is it of real practical use in day to day living?

Knowing stuff is all about memory. Actually rewind and let's put that another way - memory is all about not forgetting stuff. We come into the world knowing nothing, we leave knowing a fair amount, in between most of us will have forgotten a lot more. It's all about memory, and when it comes to dyslexics memory is perhaps the biggest conundrum of them all.

Memory is also a big subject to discuss and I can't claim to be an expert. However at a simple level it seems that there may be three basic sorts of memory - short term memory, working memory and long term memory. If you want to remember that here's a good way of looking at it:

Short term memory is like a post-it note. As your wife is rushing out of the door late for work she yells the dentist's phone number at you and asks you to call after 10.00 o'clock and book an appointment for your daughter next Saturday morning. You write it down on a post-it so you won't forget it, and keep it somewhere conspicuous where you can find it.

Working memory is when you use the info on the post-it. In this case you make the phone call using the number, speak to the dentist, book the appointment, and you've made your wife happy. If you're dyslexic of course you probably forget to write the appointment time in the calendar but hey, that wasn't in the original instructions.

However you do realise that this number might be useful in the future, so you write it down in your phone book or, being a modern sort of chap, put it in your mobile phone where it becomes a piece of long-term memory that isn't yours and can be forgotten provided you remember whether you put it under D for Dentist or the bloke's real name. Trust me, D for Dentist is safer.

So far it's all very straightforward. Go into Staples, Rymans or any other good stationers however, check out the post-it note section, and you'll find that post-it notes come in all shapes and sizes. If you're dyslexic chances are you were at the back of the queue when the big post-its were handed out, all that was left when you got there were the tiddlers.

Let's deconstruct the number of things you need to get into your 'working' memory to carry out your wife's request:

1. Find a post-it note
2. Find a pen
3. Here's a phone number
4. Write it down
5. It's for a dentist
6. Ring that dentist
7. After 10 o'clock
8. Today
9. Make appointment
10. For daughter
11. Next Saturday
12. Morning

Even if you've got a super-jumbo-bonus-pack post-it memory that's a fair bit of stuff to work with. Speaking as a fully paid-up small post-it dyslexic myself my starting point for this would always be point 7 - if I just get to remember there is something I have to do after 10 o'clock I at least have a chance of working out the rest. Most non-dyslexics would probably make the call at 10.05. In my case I generally remember point 7 whilst walking the dogs after lunch and have to hope it stays there until I get back home at 3.00 so I can make the call before the wife gets back.

The long-term memory bit is also interesting. The only thing you might ever usefully need for future reference is the dentist's phone number. You don't even need to remember the appointment time as once you've booked it you can always call and check if you've

The memory curve – regular stimulus

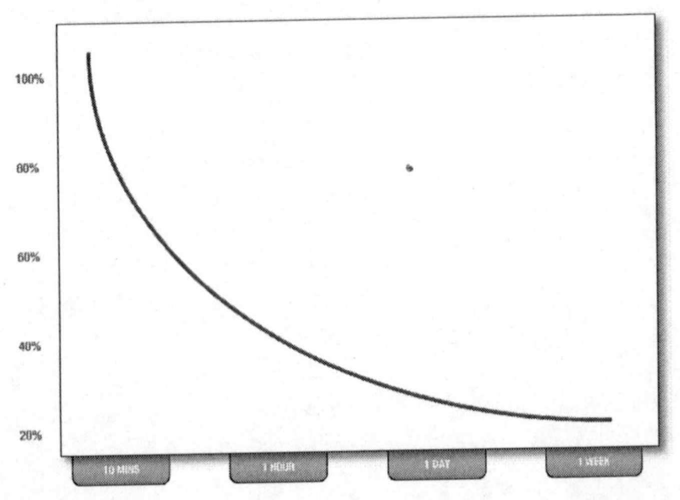

got the number. We don't need to remember a lot of what we do. Long-term memory can often afford to be selective - anyway that's my excuse and I'm sticking to it.

The forgetfulness conundrum

Here's a philosophical conundrum for you - can you forget something if you haven't remembered it in the first place? According to several past girlfriends you can!

Two things really help memory - frequency and repetition. Repeat something several times and you're more likely to remember it and develop automaticity. Repeat something several times, and then repeat it again several times soon after, and you'll perform even better. Tiger Woods doesn't spend hours on the golf range hitting balls, and David Beckham doesn't practice endless free kicks for fun - they put in the practice so they don't forget how to do it.

There is a really interesting thing called the forgetfulness curve that suggests most people need to repeat something five times, over a period of time, before they finally get it stuck in their memory.

The forgetfulness curve

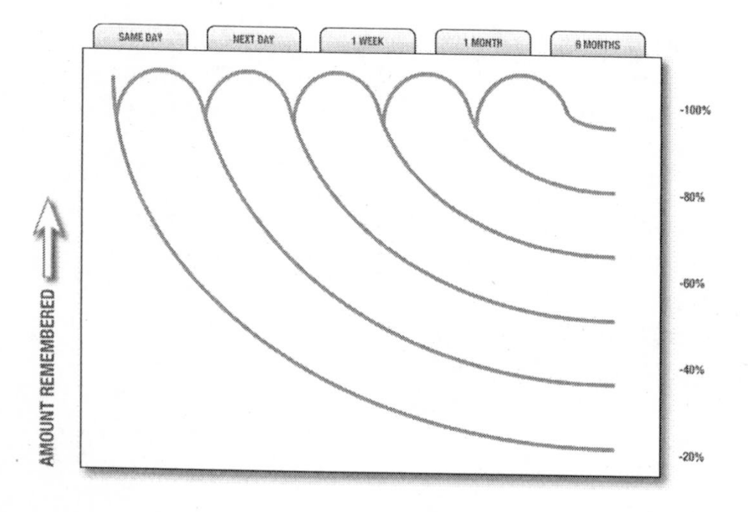

Even at my age, when I don't learn too much every day, the fact that the further away we are in time from the point of learning, the more likely we are to forget it, is something of a no-brainer. In an environment where people are continually taking in new stuff hour upon hour (such as school) it's even more obvious - you don't get time to remember the first thing before you're being asked to remember the second. By the time you get to tea-time everything before lunch is a mystery.

People naturally forget, and the more they have to remember the more they forget. Of course some people are much better at remembering than others, and actually most people can remember a shed load of stuff given time and the presentation that most suits their learning style and memory. Time is the important thing - for some of us learning not to forget something takes longer.

Author's aside
Having now got to the end of this I've added a response to my every day communication with people on occasions when they say to me 'don't tell me you've forgotten what you said/did/thought'. It's a simple line, either a statement: 'I didn't realise I needed to remember that', or a question 'did I really need to remember that?'

People often accuse others of having a 'selective memory'. Perhaps when you haven't got a good memory you naturally select and prioritise the things that you need to remember over those you don't.

When I was a lad people used to take 7 year apprenticeships to 'learn a trade'. The learning process was based on repetition and frequency. They took that long because the people who had learned before them reckoned it took that long to achieve automaticity. You kept on practising laying bricks until you could do it in your sleep and do it perfectly. Some people learned it in 5 years, some only took 3 but some took 9. We're back to our bell-shaped curve (or median!) again.

Again when I was a lad we used to learn like that at school - reciting our alphabet and our 'times tables' again and again until we could recite them perfectly. We didn't need to understand the underlying concept of codified numerics because as long as we knew what 6 x 9 came to we got a star.

We had one master at my primary school, a real disciplinarian, who started every morning with a 'times tables' test he recorded into an old fashioned reel-to-reel tape recorder. It was called 'learning by rote', which the dictionary describes as 'by mechanical or habitual repetition'.

Learning by rote sort of went out of fashion big time in the final enlightened educational decades of the last century. Educationalists preferred to think that knowledge that came from understanding was more important than knowledge for knowledge sake.

I may be wrong here, but if you think the 'mechanical and habitual repetition' of rote learning looks awfully like the 'machine like way that is consistently repetitive in response to a given stimulus' definition of the automaticity we strive for and need, I'm on your side.

The 'lesson you'll never forget' conundrum

Mr Roberts, the authoritarian primary school teacher, never ever got on with the kinaesthetic right-brained fidgety child he sat in the front row to keep a close eye on. I held the school record for being slapped on the hand with a ruler and the backside with a white plimsoll. Sometimes it was simply for fidgeting, a lot of the time it was for being forgetful. Those being the days of corporal punishment it was something of an accolade. I can't say I'm any the worse for it.

Before administering every beating Mr Roberts would tell me he was going to teach me a lesson I wouldn't forget. So I grew up associating learning with pain, or more importantly associating forgetting stuff with pain.

In many respects some things never change. Forget you were meant to be home for dinner at 7 and come back from the pub at 8 and it's a painful experience. Forget you promised to take the kids to see The Little Mermaid and it's a painful experience. Forget your anniversary - and you've guessed it.

One of the biggest problems of being a dyslexic man is that there tend to be more dyslexic men than women. Chances are we're going to end up with partners who remember everything you say. Non-dyslexic women love the charm and impulsiveness of dyslexic men but then get frustrated by them. Certainly from the moment my wife realised I was dyslexic life became much easier. She finally understood that I wasn't being lazy, wilful or disrespectful when I forgot stuff.

The lazy and wilful conundrum

Whilst hopefully we're still on the same page I'll repeat my earlier assertion that the most common symptom of dyslexia, especially in children, is underperforming against an expectation created by apparent intelligence.

Understandably your typical non-dyslexic teacher can struggle with this - if you have a child who appears bright and has good verbal skills, but then 'refuses to learn' or who 'won't pay attention and put it down on paper' it is truly a conundrum. Traditionally the obvious conclusions to draw were that the child was:

1. *Lazy*
2. *Wilful*
3. *Disruptive*
4. *Stupid*
5. *A combination of any of the above*

Do lazy and wilful children really exist? Most children are by nature inquisitive and eager to please. Dyslexic children often start out to be the opposite of lazy - they have to work harder to keep up. Problems arise when they start to get disheartened and discouraged. Walk down any supermarket aisle on a Saturday and you'll see any amount of wilful and disruptive behaviour from young children who are just crying out for attention.

The 'lazy and wilful' thing is made worse by the fact that dyslexics have trouble doing the same thing twice in the same way, and that their performance one day may not be anywhere near as good as their performance the day before. We tend to forget from one day to the next, or one time to the next, how we did it or even what we did.

Which brings us back to automaticity.

The automaticity conundrum part 2

At the age of almost 56 I have yet to learn how to use the Sky remote control properly or work an excel spread sheet. Every time I have to deal with either more than once I have to relearn how to work it and end up doing it a different way. This often ends up infuriating the people around me. The problem? I've never learned to do it by rote. Nobody has ever trained me.

It's a similar situation when it comes to building Ikea flat pack furniture. You go and buy a bookcase, bring it home, and put it together. If you have the sort of dyslexic mind Freddie has, one that sees things and shapes in 3D and puts them all together almost like an exploded CAD computer screen no problems. Unfortunately my dyslexia doesn't work for me that way.

Anyway you build it, put it against the wall, admire it, and your wife says those fateful words: 'that looks really nice, do you think we could have another one in the hallway?' Bugger! Not only do you have to schlep back to Ikea, once you've got the new one you have to start to build it all over again. And I really mean 'all over again' -

no way can I remember the order I built the first one in.

So teacher, please never assume that because a dyslexic child can do something on Monday he or she will be able to do it the same or equally as well on Tuesday. Lots of tasks simply don't come automatically to us. Hence the 7 year apprenticeship where you repeat things often enough until you can do them in your sleep.

Actually it's fascinating seeing a dyslexic child trying to sort out a computer. They tend to have an approach that can only be called 'hacking'. Non-dyslexic computer boffins always go through a tried and tested process. Dyslexics make huge cognitive jumps around the motherboard based on their own mental wiring. Often it's a lot faster.

The memory versus learning conundrum

It seems to me that you can't remember something unless you've learned it, and you haven't learned anything unless you've memorised it. If knowledge is the stuff you've got stuck in your head perhaps education and teaching would be more effective if everything focused on techniques for memorising things before we were expected to learn the facts.

The brain conundrum

The brain is a conundrum right from the start. The left hand hemisphere of the brain controls the right hand side of the body. The right hand hemisphere does the opposite. Humans are joined-up, or rather we are designed to be joined-up, 'cross laterally'. Even more strange is that in a non-dyslexic brain the left hemisphere is always bigger than the right, whilst in a dyslexic brain both hemispheres tend to be the same size. Research suggests that this is because the right hemisphere is larger, rather than the left hemisphere being smaller.

This strikes me as particularly bizarre. Look closely at any drop-dead gorgeous woman or stunningly good looking man and you realise that the world values bi-lateral symmetry really highly. Things that are perfectly balanced look good. For purposes of self-esteem I shall believe then that we 10% have drop-dead gorgeous brains - and that in time we learn to do beautiful things.

For some reason the cross-lateral plot of nature is a pretty important part of normality. Dyslexics typically have very poor cross lateral linkages in their brain, which means that when one hemisphere needs to talk to the other there can be a roaring silence. This has all sorts of impacts, some as simple as being clumsy when younger. I was forever being told off for running into things and dropping things.

Freddie's dyslexia is typical of this. How proud were we as parents when Freddie didn't crawl but at an early age got to his feet and walked in a small and perfectly formed fashion? Very! How wrong were we? Extremely!

Crawling, that is putting your right hand and left knee forward at the same time, and vice-versa, is an important or even vital step in forging those cross-lateral pathways.

Actually we know a lot about how the brain works these days. Different bits look after different things - you can see this by using FMRI scans to see which bits of the grey matter 'light up' when you're doing different stuff.

Another author's aside here - I happen to know from being a copywriter that FMRI stands for Funtioning Magnetic Resonance Imaging. I also know that CAT in CAT scanning stands for Computer Aided Tomotography. Bizarrely lots of people who daily use the terms MRI and CAT couldn't tell you that. Whilst I don't know how either work I know when to use the names. Not that I drop the words into many dinner party conversations. Funny thing education and knowledge.

Compare an FMRI scan of a dyslexic brain when speaking, reading, or doing a whole host of other things, with that of a non-dyslexic brain, and it lights up in completely different places, or even doesn't light up at all. In particular when the brain is involved with things to do with speech and language the areas that light up in a non-dyslexic brain are in the left hemisphere, but the areas that light up in the dyslexic brain are in the right one as well and much more random. When it comes to memory, especially short-term and working memory, the non-dyslexic brain lights up like the Blackpool illuminations whilst the dyslexic brain sputters like an Ikea tea-light.

The dyslexic brain may have a lot more power under the hood but it sure wasn't around when they were handing out the big boot space. The fact is that 'stuff' has to go through the short-term memory to get filed away into the long-term memory. A big boot means you might only need one journey to get a lot of stuff from one place to the other. With a small boot you have to make a lot of small repeated journeys to ensure it all arrives safely. That is why we have to work harder and keep on repeating stuff over and again until we've 'learned' it.

The left/right/mid-brainer conundrum

Talk to people working in the field of dyslexia and they will commonly refer to each other, and particularly themselves, as 'left-brained' or 'right-brained'. Listen carefully and you suddenly realise that the playground rules from your childhood days are completely reversed - a lot of self-confessed and assessed left-brained people might secretly rather be right-brained.

This is nature working her mischief yet again. When we are young we want to conform. As we get older we want to differentiate. It's as if we have to prove we can do all the stuff everybody else can do before we can show what's special about us. Once again it's a lot to do with what we value as success.

Left-brained people function particularly well in many walks of life. They handle life's processes without hesitation. They have very efficient filing cabinets in their heads, they have orderly minds, and they know where to look for the stuff they have filed away and how to retrieve it. This is the slightly 'grey' side of the grey matter with the brain working as a super-computer and what goes in comes out the same way. Fabulous if you want to be an accountant or work in admin.

But could a computer ever write Beethoven's Fifth symphony, or Hamlet, or Harry Potter? It seems that when it comes to imagination and creativity the right side of the dyslexic brain goes off like a solar powered kaleidoscope in the Sahara sun while the non-dyslexic right hemisphere urgently needs new batteries.

Creative people, innovators and even sports people who perform at a high level tend to be right-brained. When we go to the filing cabinet we can't find what we thought we were looking for, or more probably can't remember where we put it, so we rummage around, pull out whatever we can get our hands on and cobble something new and different together. We might make a hell of a mess of the filing system but that doesn't matter as we wouldn't know where to look for it all again anyway. The point is the end result may just be a thing of remarkable beauty and originality.

In reality very few people are wholly left or wholly right-brained although most of us favour one side or the other. One of the very best things of all about the brain is that it is brilliant at compensating for problems. So once it's worked out we have challenges in accessing the speech and language centres of the left hemisphere, and, if we work hard enough to exercise it, it forges links and even grows bigger in some areas to make links easier.

Making the brain work this hard often gives you the feeling of your mind being boggled as you try to get your head round stuff.

Typically you feel this in the frontal lobes. I particularly get it when trying to work out 3D stuff or flat pack furniture - my brain actively hurts. Often the brain doesn't seem to work its way around stuff first time up, but if you sleep on it you can be amazed what it can do.

Perhaps that's the really brilliant thing about being a dyslexic - if I could write a mantra that every dyslexic should have stuck on the bathroom mirror to read every morning if would be something like this:

Alright, so my brain doesn't work the same way most people's do. The great thing for me is that it's clever enough to help me work out how to compensate so I can learn to do all the things everybody else can, just as well as they do, if I work hard. The sad thing for everybody else is they'll probably never be able to learn to do half the things that come really easily to me.

Because dyslexics have to make their brain work harder we get more out of them.

That's almost enough of the brain from me. There are heaps of excellent books on it and if you want to find out more the one I've dipped into, albeit lightly in dyslexic fashion, is called 'Teaching the brain to read' by Dr. Duncan Milne. If you pick it up don't be put off by all the hard words, it's got lots of easily accessible diagrams.

The learner's conundrum

The accepted term in the education business for a young person put in a position where they are expected to take in knowledge-based communication is 'a learner'. To my mind this puts the onus of effort, and responsibility for success, on the child.

If they don't 'learn' presumably it's their fault. It could of course be the fault of the teacher - but then again the teacher has been professionally 'trained' whereas the learner is de facto a blank canvas, an empty bottle, an ingenue. In this situation any apparent failure to transfer the knowledge from teacher to learner looks certain to be the learner's fault, especially if the teacher is succeeding with 9 out of 10 other learners.

Once again, as dyslexics, let's get real about this. If the teacher is getting it right nine out of ten times then that's a 90% strike rate. Given that the very best multi-million pound strikers in the football league premiership only score in 50% of their games, 90% is a tremendous achievement.

So this then is the dyslexic learner's conundrum, aged 7: 'everybody says how bright I am, I'm talkative and have a good vocabulary, I get on well with my peers and they seem to like me, adults think I'm interesting, then mummy and daddy take me to school where I can tell I'm brighter than a lot of the other kids, I really do 'get it' when teacher tells me things - but I can't seem to learn to read or write or spell and put it on paper even though some of the less interesting kids find it easy'.

In a common parlance dyslexic kids can 'talk the talk' but can't 'walk the walk'. More specifically they can't 'read the read' or 'write the write'.

Kids want to conform. Dyslexic kids would much rather be like the other 90%. At first they don't understand why they're different - why should they? Until the world formally assesses how different we are we're all guessing anyway. On this basis the learner's conundrum is simply 'I want to keep up, why can't I, how do I do it?'

Faced with this situation a common outcome is frustration that often manifests itself as bad behaviour. Disruptive behaviour leads to being labelled as a 'problem'. Without a solution, being a 'problem' becomes the only claim to peer group fame a child may have. Before long it can become a vicious spiral.

At the other end of the spectrum is another common outcome - the child simply gives up trying. When I used to ask Freddie how he was getting on with spelling he would say 'that's something older boys do'. He wasn't prepared to attempt it for fear of embarrassment as that was the easier route. Yet how often do we learn by getting things wrong first?

The summer conundrum

Age should never be underrated as a factor in dyslexia. My two kids were born in May and July - they were summer babies and always amongst the youngest in their year, or cohort. For them, comparison with people in the same school year was never going to be a level playing field. On Fred's 10th birthday there were people in his year nearly 10% older than him.

Give anybody a 10m start in a hundred yard race and it's going to be tough to beat them - even if they have no other abnormalities. I don't know that there are any statistics that suggest dyslexic children are more likely to be born at a specific time of year (perhaps I'll do a star sign survey). I was born in September and was always one of the oldest in my year. However if you have a summer born child you think (or know) is dyslexic then be prepared.

There is another summer factor that should also be taken into account - hay fever. Research shows dyslexia is often closely linked to deficiencies in the auto-immune system. Dyslexics are much more prone to allergies and I'm a slave to hay fever drugs myself. A summer born dyslexic child with hay fever, taking exams in the height of the pollen season, is never going to perform to true potential.

The mentors' conundrum

Those who mentor children through the formative years, parents and teachers alike, need to be honest with dyslexic kids. Don't try to hide from them the fact it's going to be tough. Be honest and tell them 'you're going to have to work a bit harder but you're going to get there'. One of the great things about having an assessment is that you have the security of establishing an IQ and knowing what centile that puts them on. You can share their true potential with them.

If your child has an IQ that puts him or her on the 80th centile you can genuinely tell them on days when things look dark that in their school of 500 they are in the top 100 brightest people. Tell them to be patient. Tell them it will work out. Having a high IQ tends to kick-in when those with less power in the engine start to slow down - rather like a stagger unwinding on the bend of a 400m race when those who might look in front may well come last.

Most of all be positive. I'm told that beautiful women look in the mirror and only see the blemishes. Kids are no different. As a qualified cricket coach I came to realise that kids focus on the lows and not on the highs. In doing so what they miss is all the 'really OK stuff' around the middle.

The single most useful piece of coaching dialogue I developed was 'what's wrong with that then?' This, or the alternative 'look, there's nothing wrong with that', would be delivered to bowlers after a good ball that the batsman hadn't scored off, or to batsmen who had kept a good ball out.

Emotionally neither player thought he had succeeded. The simple fact is that batsmen naturally expect to get a four off every ball and bowlers expect a wicket with every ball. Life is simply not like that and just because you didn't succeed it doesn't mean you've failed. There's a lot of good solid stuff in the middle that is essential but goes unnoticed - mentors need to start noticing the middle ground and recognising it as an achievement.

Self-esteem is important for everybody and especially dyslexics. There are few things more frustrating than knowing something in your head but not being able to put it on a piece of paper. Many adult dyslexics, when they are finally assessed, feel this great sense of relief and some even comment that they thought they might be going mad.

Find something or some things your child is good at and praise them. It may be sport, it may be playing the drums, it may be doing tricks on a bike, it may be painting Warhammer figures, or playing Halo 3 or Guitar Hero on the X-Box. Celebrate and reward it - we don't need to be good at everything.

The language conundrum

Language is essential for communication. Why we don't speak the same language all around the world is perhaps the biggest conundrum there is - wouldn't it make life easier if, like Ford Prefect in The Hitch Hikers Guide to the Galaxy we could put a 'Babel fish' in our ear and understand every word everybody said. As anybody who has double-ordered cabbage by mistake in a Croatian restaurant will tell you, it would be certainly be very useful.

Language is controlled by the brain and the bizarre fact is that all around the world brains don't differ very much. The language centre in a native Japanese speaking person will be more or less in the same place and function the same way as that of an English speaking person.

Languages vary enormously and learning to speak them is a rather complicated process. Learning to translate what you hear into visual coded symbols (writing) and then translate those coded symbols back into speech (reading) is even more complicated. It's an almost totally multi-layered event using all the senses apart from smell.

The key to the process is phonics - translating the sounds into symbols and back again. Different languages are more phonetic than others, and generally the more phonetic the language - i.e. the more regular and rigid the sound and symbols stay - the easier it is for dyslexics to learn.

French may be a beautiful language to listen to but it's a hopeless language for most dyslexics and my two really struggled. It would have been much easier if they could have taken Spanish or Latin where the letters always have the same sound. However the curriculum is the curriculum.

English is a language full of conundrums. That grand old man of letters George Bernard Shaw once worked out a phonic spelling of the word 'fish' as 'GHOTI'.

- 'gh' from the word tough sounds like 'f'
- 'o' from the word 'women' sounds like 'i'
- 'ti' from the word 'nation' sounds like 'sh'

Obviously our George was between plays that day, but it does point out the challenges we dyslexics face. Lots of words in English simply have to be remembered. Some you can work out phonetically, but others are completely illogical.

The reading conundrum

The brain was not designed to read. For centuries the spoken word was enough - reading was not essential to survival, so we didn't need to bother.

Having said that the act of turning the spoken word into symbols, so we could record stuff and share it on a one-to-many basis, may well be the biggest technological advance mankind has ever made. Certainly without it no other major technological advance would have been possible.

Reading has become a necessity. We live in a world where not being able to read can be positively dangerous. For instance we are surrounded by health and safety experts who put up written signs telling us what we can and cannot do. If we can't read that a walnut cake may contain traces of nuts we could be in all sorts of trouble.

Seriously though reading offers a major shortcut to the acquisition of knowledge. One expert writes something down, thousands more can acquire the wisdom at a distance. Books, magazines, newspapers, websites - we live in a world driven by information and explanation.

Reading rarely features on the top five favourite pastimes of dyslexics. Having written this however I now immediately question it as there are plenty of older dyslexics I know who, like me, are quite passionate readers. In my mind this can only be due to the fact we were taught by rote and had 'English Language' drilled into us in Sergeant Majorly fashion.

The vocabulary conundrum

A big conundrum for those who have to work with dyslexic children is the fact that we dyslexics tend to have a vocabulary well advanced for our age. We can surprise and delight adults with the words we use, and equally importantly the way we use them, and even when young our powers of reasoning and argument can seem impressive.

Armed with a big vocabulary, and having learned to read strictly phonically and by rote, with 'sounding-out' techniques deeply ingrained, is a great recipe for any inquisitive dyslexic (and most of us are at least that) to become a voracious reader.

Modern day dyslexics try and write down the good words they know and fail completely - and this inability to harness in writing the words we want to use to communicate our ideas and feelings can be yet another source of frustration and low self-esteem. And yet another reason to give up, or at least give in for a bit.

Our seeming facility to communicate well vocally, linked closely with the inability to read, write and spell the words we are using, should be seen as a motorway junction sized signpost on the journey through education saying 'assess this child for dyslexia now!' Ignore it at your peril as it demonstrates the intelligence of comprehension aligned with a large disconnect in the language department of the brain.

Perhaps we dyslexics are a throw back to those medieval times when the articulate person was highly valued, when the warmest spot next to the fire in winter was reserved for the story-teller. If so give me a time machine now and start mulling the ale.

Alternatively perhaps we simply haven't evolved. It does strike me as strange that even though the brain wasn't designed to read and write it's a skill a large percentage of the population pick up in a quite straightforward manner. It's almost as if the latent skill was there in most people waiting to be developed. Like Thursday's child (and I am one) perhaps nature meant us to work hard for a living.

The writing conundrum

You don't need to be able to write to survive. Indeed the vast majority of the population write hardly anything once they stop taking exams. The written word for a vast number of people need go no further than filling in forms - and you can normally find someone to do that for you - and signing your name.

Speaking as a writer it's weird to think that one of the first things we all learn to do is write. Most people can write to a greater or lesser degree, but 50 years on from the day I first sat in a classroom, writing has been a skill that has kept me in a half-decent living. Actually the same is true of counting - if you're any good at numbers you can become an accountant and rule the world.

In truth the writing conundrum is a bit of side show in this discussion. There are some people that actually can't make meaningful marks on paper (known in the trade as 'dysgraphics') but they are few and far between. The real problems facing most dyslexics is getting the right letters the right way round and then getting them in the right order.

The transposition conundrum

We were watching one of those Anne Robinson 'Test the Nation' quizzes one night on TV and they came to a series of those visual questions where you had to fit a reasonably complicated shaped piece into the right shaped hole. I was useless at it, Freddie was brilliant. To his dyslexic brain a shape is a shape whether it's upside down or back to front. If shape fitting ever comes to the Olympics Freddie is in a podium position. Likewise when building flat-pack furniture becomes a recognised event - we should have him sponsored by Ikea.

It's not the same however when it comes to the letters 'b', 'd', 'p' and even 'q'. The only saving grace 'q' has is that it's invariably followed by a 'u' which makes a 'qu' shape. Don't even mention 'g' which in this typeface looks alright, but which in blackboard writing can morph into other things all too easily.

To a dyslexic brain they all look the same as you simply have one shape re-arranged differently in the same space. To non-dyslexics of course they all look completely individual and represent unique sounds. Although if you sound them out to yourself now (don't do this on a train or a bus) you must admit the sounds are pretty similar. Well, I think so.

The vision conundrum

I want to slightly 'go off on one' here and talk a bit about semantics. More accurately I probably want to talk about 'epistemology' but that just sounds a bit poncey. Skip the next paragraph if you want before reading on.

The point about knowledge is we all have to agree to describe things in the same way. Naming things is important. But what if we don't all see things the same way? We all call red 'red' because that's what we've learned to call it. However nobody knows if what I see as red is what you see as green - we still call it red anyway. Demonstrably however when it comes to minding our 'p's and our 'q's not everybody sees things the same way.

Language and convention suggest that we all see the same things in the same way. Science suggests that perhaps we don't. Back in the day dyslexia started off being called 'Word Blindness'. The first dedicated efforts in researching and helping people who had problems was at a place called 'The Word Blind Institute'. The main assumption then was that some people simply didn't see letters and words in the same way. Some still don't.

There is growing awareness of the science of Behavioural Optometry - that is the way people's eyes work in practice and what they actually see. There is a lot of evidence that suggests that some dyslexic's eyes see things in a different or slower way - letters seem to jump around.

A large proportion of dyslexics struggle to read black type on a white page. Our daughter Phoebe reads best when she puts a yellow-coloured acetate overlay on top of the page. Others prefer blue or green. A couple of years ago I did a website for a specialist dyslexia school where you could change the colour of the type and the background. Cream on blue works particularly well so that's how we designed the logo.

Once again it comes back to the fact that the dyslexic brain is wired differently - and that can simply mean anything as no two dyslexic brains will be wired the same.

The hearing conundrum

The ability to hear things takes practice. It's a loud world out there with a huge amount of noise. Being able to distinguish one sound from another really is a huge skill, but one which most people take for granted.

Once you can hear and distinguish sounds then there should be no reason why you can't link them to a graphic shape - providing you don't see some shapes as all the same! But what if you can't hear them in the first place?

A lot of dyslexics have, or have had, hearing problems. Grommets in the ears feature regularly in the history of dyslexic children.

It's a strange thing, listening. Most people are bad at it. I was very lucky to have a Dad who had been a musician who had played the clarinet and violin. From a very early age - probably four - Sunday morning was devoted to listening to music, with my Dad asking me to pick out the various instruments.

It's a wonderful thing to do, and to this day I can sit in a concert and isolate the French Horn or Oboe or Second Violas. The one thing I cannot do is translate what I'm hearing to written music or vice versa. Try as I might, and believe me I have, I can no more read notes on a stave than neuter cats. Both attempts would produce similar sounds.

Listening is yet another memory skill. Sounds have to go through short term memory to get into the long term filing department. Then we not only have to be able to retrieve them individually, we need to be able to work out what they sound like when they sit next to other sounds. It's no easy task and to compound it we don't make the same sounds in the same language in different parts of the country. Go to the Yorkshire Dales or Newcastle and you'll find completely different pronunciations of the same word.

The slow processing conundrum

Our senses are brilliant at giving us information - go them, that's what they're there for. However we don't all process the same information at the same speed. As dyslexics we might have a turbo-charged 4 litre diesel engine under the bonnet but we're still going to miss out on a fast break at the lights for the first mile against a 150cc Vespa scooter.

In computer terms this is all about the difference between your RAM and your ROM. Let's face it you're not going to send a rocket to the moon from your average laptop. Then again you probably wouldn't need to use your IBM Mainframe to send an email.

In part this is because, even if we have learned good strategies to compensate for our individual learning styles, it can take us a little longer to understand the question, and rummage round in the filing cabinets of the mind for the bits we need to come up with the right answer.

Whilst we're rummaging the neat and tidy minds of the non-dyslexics will have opened the right drawer first time and come up with exactly the same solution they always do - just like a good computer should. Meanwhile our randomly wired computers are busily hacking through piles of random facts until we decide we can't remember where we put what we're looking for so we'll be inventive and work with what we've got to find the best answer we can.

Inventive, now there's a good word for dyslexics. Slow and inventive - three more good words. Interestingly the words 'fast' and 'inventive' rarely seem to go together unless you're Doctor Who - then again he's got a sonic screwdriver and Time on his side. Actually I'm betting that dyslexia is a state of normality for Gallefre-itians anyway.

Author's aside
This is totally bizarre but I've just opened this document on a Thursday morning expecting to find the 2,000 odd words I wrote yesterday, mostly on the train. For some reason I forgot to save them - which as a professional writer is most unlike me. I have no way of remembering what I wrote and only a vague recollection of what the headings were. So from here on in I'm having to write it all again. I wonder what I said, and if what I say now will be anything like the first draft. Oh well, if I end up repeating things I wrote earlier, please excuse me, I'll try and take repetition out at the editing stage.

The comprehension conundrum
Something that may go part of the way to explaining slow processing is the fact dyslexics tend to be very literal. In order to better understand stuff we tend to train ourselves to try and hear/recognise/encode every word. Context is vitally important to us - we use pictures or other words around the words, or facial expressions and body language, or tone of voice to give us the sense of how things are meant.

The spoken word can have many fewer contextual clues. People can deliver a passionate line with a deadpan face, and vice versa. Take context away and you may find us staring at you blankly for a few seconds whilst we run all the possible interpretations through our minds.

If you have ever lived with a dyslexic teenager you'll almost certainly have gone through what I call 'the teenage lawyer' phase where they take literally everything you say at face value. Careful how you compose that face as you speak, and choose your words with caution as the slightest mis-communication can lead to a kitchen table tribunal.

I realised this sitting at the kitchen table one day helping Freddie revise some Latin. Every sentence we read I found myself telling him 'the verb is at the end of the sentence'. After about 10 repetitions of this he asked me 'Daddy, is the verb 'always' at the end of the sentence in Latin?' I missed one vital word - always. Then again the fact his slow processing mind worked it out by itself means he'll remember it for life - not that he'll ever need to, but that's education. Or rather knowledge.

The spelling conundrum

If the brain wasn't initially designed to read or write it certainly wasn't designed to spell. Yet the ability to spell seems to have become the badge of accepted intelligence. If you don't spell something right people (classmates and teachers alike) laugh at you and say you're stupid.

On the one hand the fact that getting a group of letters in the right order is more important than the ideas or words you are writing down is absurd. On the other I suppose good spelling is one of man's higher intellectual achievements. The fact remains that the term 'illiterate' is synonymous with 'unintelligent' or even worse.

None of this mattered until Samuel Johnson sat down in a Fleet Street coffee house and wrote the first dictionary, at the same time stultifying the English language and consigning dyslexics to the dunce's corner for centuries to come. Hmmm, 'd' is for dunce and 'd' is for dyslexia - now there's a thought. Of course as far as most dyslexics were concerned the 'd' could equally have been a 'p' or a 'b'.

Pre-Johnson, in the days of those great men of literature Chaucer and Shakespeare, the same word was often spelled several different ways within the same text forsooth. Luckily for young Geoffrey and Will the naughty step hadn't been invented.

Even in my day exams were as much a spelling test as any sort of attempt to find out what you knew. Sure in a subject like English it's fair enough to lose marks for spelling. But surely it's more important in the world of Geography to know what causes a Glacial Striation than to know how it's spelled.

My wife, the dyslexia specialist, is outraged by this. She points out that those who mark papers are not normally allowed to deduct more than 5% of the overall marks in any exam for poor spelling - it's much more important for dyslexic candidates to get the knowledge down than waste time worrying about spelling it right.

The 'PA' conundrum

The advent of computers and email has removed the need for many male executives to employ a PA or secretary. At the same time this has led to a massive surge in the number of adult men who have been forced to confront the fact that they are dyslexic.

For years executives worked as a team with their PA - he knew what to say and she knew how to spell it, and type it. (Please excuse any gender stereotyping here, but it's predominant with men.) In many cases this is causing problems in the middle and upper layers of business. Men who may previously have been promoted as a matter of course are facing the fact that spelling is an essential component of communication and they are being held back by it.

Just as at school this can cause problems of self-esteem. There is a great story of a brilliant scientist who was down to the short list for an impressive job but who knew the psychometric tests he had been asked to take would almost certainly give away his dyslexia.

'So tell us, why should we choose you to work here?' came the question.

'Before I answer that,' replied the applicant, 'can you tell me how many dyslexics you have on your team?'

'None that we know of,' said the chairman of the interview panel having looked around his colleagues who nodded agreement. Either he didn't know or didn't like to admit it.

'Then it's high time you had one,' the applicant said confidently. 'I'll bring a completely new perspective to the department!'

Not only did he get the job, he was very successful.

The exam conundrum

So here's the point of it all. At certain points of your life society decides the time is right to find out what you know by making you sit down, read a question and come up with an answer which you then have to write down using words in which all the letters are the right way round and in an acceptable and established order. Fair play to society, it's quite an efficient and effective way of bench-marking a cohort of young people and taking a snapshot of what they might or might not be able to go on and do for the next part of their educational careers.

Anyway dyslexics are good at coming up with answers - we're generally bright, we're natural problem solvers, we reason well and we tend to have extensive vocabulary. Surely then we should do well, shouldn't we?

Doing well sort of assumes we can work out what the question is in the first place. And that generally brings us back to reading, comprehension and processing speed. If the questions were read out loud to us, or better still delivered in a multi-sensory fashion, perhaps on a power point slide with a voice-over, we'd get off to a more certain start.

The multiple choice conundrum

The move to multiple-choice style exams has made life simple for a lot of people. At the same time it has made life hell for many dyslexics.

Suddenly we're not only faced with having to read and comprehend a question. We're then presented with four possible answers many of which mostly use the same words and even sound similar when read out loud.

Multiple choice and dyslexia became a much more high profile topic in July 2008 when a dyslexic medical student took the British Medical Association to court under the DDA (Disability Discrimination Act) claiming multiple choice exams discriminated against dyslexics. There was lots of news about it at the time, but the outcome seems not to have been reported, or is yet to come to a conclusion.

The equity conundrum

Some people might disagree with society's fascination with exams but by and large the world is a competitive sort of place and most people are happy to have their competence measured in a fair test with everybody else.

Among other things sometimes it's important in life to work out what you're not so good at in order to find out what you might be best doing next. In the big grown up track-and-field event of life some people are sprinters and some are distance runners. Some are jumpers and some are throwers. Some are better off keeping the time or measuring the distances. Equally importantly, for every person out there on the playing field you'll find any number of people in the background making sure the event takes place and runs to order.

The important thing for a fair test is that everybody should be on a level playing field. In sprinting that's easy, you all start on the same line at the same time and you can measure each individual's merits 100 metres (or 5,000m) later as they cross the line.

The fact is that in legal terms dyslexia is recognised under the 1995 DDA and employers and educationalists alike are obliged to make allowances for any "physical or mental impairment which has a substantial and long-term adverse effect on the ability to carry out normal day-to-day activities".

Whilst most of my thoughts in this essay deal with dyslexia at a young age, dyslexia is still a real problem for adults in the workplace - especially as the science of dyslexia is a relatively recent thing and many adults are never diagnosed until real discrimination or bullying happens. Google "DDA and Dyslexia" and you'll find some interesting case law and positive action on the business front - as ever professional practice in the HR and Personnel sectors of the real world seems some way in advance of education.

The other aspect of 'equity' is that it is the fundamental underlying principle of English law - the legislators start with the assumption that everybody is equal and should be judged on that basis. And quite right too, that's what civilised society should be all about.

The discrimination conundrum

When it comes to dyslexia, education and employment are polar opposites. In the work place employers have to prove that they are not discriminating and have a financial interest in doing so. They have to show their everyday practices and actions are not detrimental to an individual's prospects and that the playing field is level. If they do discriminate it costs them money.

The case in education is reversed. Here the authorities need to positively discriminate in favour of dyslexics by making arrangements and allowances to compensate. They are obliged to discriminate, and that too costs money and resources.

With pressure on resources from taxpayer's money it's no surprise that the parents and mentors of dyslexic children often need to be aggressively proactive with certain authorities and educators.

The fact that, for children of a young age, parents will generally have to fork out for an assessment, or hope to secure charitable support to fund it, suggests 'the system' is inherently dyslexic averse. At the primary age, when it's most important that dyslexia is spotted, and when most can be done to help a child to compensate, the system seems to be in denial.

Conversely by the time we get to sixth form the system starts 'screening' for dyslexia to actively seek out those who may be challenged who have not yet been spotted. The same is true when we move into higher education when once again screening, backed up by all sorts of allowances, and resources such as free laptops, suddenly seem to be available.

Perversely you can't help but wonder whether the money spent in the late teens might be better allocated to the greatest good of the greatest number in the formative years.

The extra time conundrum

The most common way to level the playing field for dyslexics sitting examinations is to allocate extra time - normally up to 25% of the length of the standard time allotted. The theory here is that extra time will address the reading, comprehension and slow processing aspects of dyslexia. Accordingly dyslexic students are advised to use the time to fully understand the questions.

It's not a bad system although even with 25% both my kids still failed to get to the end of some papers, particularly those with essay-based answers. The 'short question and answer' format seemed to suit them better. As discussed above multiple choice is something of a mixed blessing - easy enough to get to the end but a risk of confusion on the way.

In severe cases dyslexic students may be allowed to use laptops. Why they can't all do that is a complete mystery as a spell checker would remove the stress and time wasted worrying about spelling. Likewise being taught to touch type really helps writing speed. In the most extreme cases students will be allowed a 'scribe' to whom they can dictate answers. Sadly the lovely Latin word for this 'amenuensis' has gone out of fashion. Perhaps 'having an amenuensis' sounded too much like a medical emergency.

Actually there is no conundrum here at all really. The system has to respond somehow and, once it has agreed that you're dyslexic, it boldly makes as much accommodation as it reasonably can. The only risk is that for some people this may be 'too much too late' but all the more reason to get assessed as early as possible.

The only conundrum that does occur to me here is that dyslexics never seem to bond as a group. As a matter of course I used to ask my kids how many other people were being awarded extra time and who were they - generally they didn't seem to notice.

As dyslexia is spotted later rather than sooner the number of students allowed extra time naturally increases year on year but even so it seems dyslexics don't recognise each other or share a kindred spirit. I have yet to come across a school or other place of education with a 'dyslexia club'.

The passage of time conundrum

In most respects time is the greatest leveller of all. Technology may help but time is of the essence. First of all we dyslexics must invest time in ourselves, and the more effort we put into developing strategies to compensate for our strangely wired brains the greater the rewards we reap.

However it's a long and frustrating journey. To keep motivated along the route we need other people - parents, teachers and mentors - to invest time as well. Plus large dollops of emotional support when it seems like things are going nowhere.

Finally we need 'the system' to invest time in the way of patience, and time taken to re-evaluate our progress on a regular basis. We're a needy lot, but we respect the input and time of others. I hope we reward it too.

The first impression conundrum

There is a great saying that 'you only get one chance at making a first impression' and it's very true. It's human nature to pigeon-hole individuals at first glance and treat them accordingly from then on. Education is no exception and we are grouped together or 'streamed' according to an expectation that is often passed on from one school or teacher to the next.

Whilst Freddie had some serious challenges we were always confident he would, in the fullness of time, overcome them. By the time he was ready to move to senior school he was starting to get reasonable grades in some subjects. He was good at sciences, Geography, RE and other things where reasoning rather than regurgitation were at a premium.

However, when he moved up to senior school, they 'set' students solely on their ability in French. As mentioned above French may be the language of love but it's not the language of dyslexics. Based on this particular 'first impression' he ended up in some classes that were well below his ability or the speed he wanted to work at.

At the same time being in these sets meant the school expectation, even up to his final pre-GCSE report, was that he'd get B and C grades. At the end of the day he did get one C - for French! The other 10 were all A or A*. Like the stagger unwinding in a 400 metre race he may have looked behind for a long time but hit the front when it mattered.

Actually underneath it all he was pretty confident he could get top grades - but the continuing dumbing-down of the expectation from his teachers was not good for his self-esteem. Perhaps sometimes teachers don't know everything, then again they have a classroom full of students to look after whilst a parent has a singular focus. And they're probably safer for managing expectations down rather than up.

The politics and policy conundrum

I'm now just about at the end of the 20,000 words I thought I might write. Looking back over the preceding pages I'm not quite sure what I've achieved other than to perhaps point out that there are different types of dyslexias and memories and brains and intelligencies. And that we dyslexics are a complicated, unpredictable and somewhat contrary bunch. Hopefully you'll have a more rounded view of us.

When I started I thought I'd end up by having a pop at the system for not taking our challenges more seriously. However as I've gone through my thoughts I'm coming to think that we're lucky that some of the 90% go to so much trouble to help us.

On the one hand, in comparison to the 90% of normal people, dyslexics are extremely high maintenance. On the other, if you catch us early and leverage our many and varied talents for problem solving and innovation, we perform at a high level and offer a big payback. The cost-benefit of supporting a dyslexic is not a sum I feel particularly inclined to do. I hope over time it would come out with a positive bottom line.

Then again you can't just leave 10% of children out on a hillside overnight to see if they survive. Then again you can't easily lump all that 10% together and treat us the same way - the most general output for a dyslexic child is the development of an Individual Education Plan (or IEP) which means we have to be considered one at a time and in all probability taught as such.

All I can repeat is that, from the sanity point of view, with most of the world now going on to higher education of some format, and given the knowledge that dyslexics are bright enough to compensate over time, it could well be worth diverting the resources allocated to discovering and accommodating dyslexics at higher education to assessment and remedial activity in the formative years.

It would of course be excellent within the broader economy if the system could fund assessments for all those who appeared to be dyslexic. Special needs costs aside I feel there must be a significant collateral benefit to be delivered by reducing the parental stress and time involved.

The lifetime of dyslexia conundrum

I have no wish for this essay to appear to be a bleeding heart apology for dyslexics. But we do work hard to get there, and some of us get to infinity and beyond. And we do so in spite of being dyslexic for all of our lives. We're dyslexic when we're born, and we'll be equally as dyslexic the day we die.

So it's not like being ill and recovering. There is no miracle cure or drug we can take to make it better. Becoming a 'well compensated' dyslexic, hopefully so well compensated most of the people around us most of the time suspect we might actually be normal, is the result of a lot of effort from a lot of people.

If you're one of those people who supports and helps dyslexics then on behalf of us all 'thank you' - we'll be thankful all our lives.

If you have a child who is dyslexic then keep the faith. The light at the end of the tunnel is most definitely switched on, burning bright and will go on getting ever closer until one day your child will emerge brilliantly.

If you are an adult and feel you may be an undiagnosed dyslexic you are certainly not alone and help and understanding are out there. You're never too old to be a dyslexic, or have an assessment.

Finally, if you have a dyslexic in your family, or one who is a friend, be proud of them and celebrate their differences.

Appendices

I'm never sure about writing anything that has the same name as a useless fold of skin that dangles south somewhere about the junction of the small and large intestines. There are however a few things I want to add that don't really fit in with the main narrative of this essay. Mainly some case study type stuff about how we worked out dyslexia was a family trait, how it was diagnosed and how it impacted on us.

As you probably expect mostly it's about the wisdom of hindsight, in the hope that my hindsight can act as the foresight for others. Until you start to suspect that one of your children may be dyslexic, or that indeed you yourself may be dyslexic, there's lots of both denial and guesswork going on. Hopefully these last few bits may take out some of that guesswork.

Appendix 1 - the Phoebe conundrum

I haven't written much about my daughter Phoebe, although in fact it was because of her that we came to realise we were dyslexic. More specifically it's due to a certain Mrs Gill David, who was Phoebe's A level history teacher to whom thanks are due.

Phoebe had always been a very forward and bright girl. She reached the normal walking and talking milestones as you would expect. Language wasn't a problem for her, although she speaks very quickly and is not always intelligible. We lived just outside Richmond in South West London and she went to a good state primary school where Phoebe was an apt pupil.

As she was such a bright and interested person, and extremely inquisitive, we took her to a Montessori nursery before she started primary. With the way that Montessori works it's fair to say she started learning skills to compensate for her dyslexia there. Good for her self-esteem, but it may have kept the dyslexia hidden for longer.

The local ambition for everybody with a bright daughter was that she would get into the excellent Tiffin Girls School in Kingston. Accordingly Phoebe had extra coaching to enable her to sit the quite exacting entrance exam. Within the state system she did admirably in her SATs. She sang the lead in *Joseph and the Amazing Technicolour Dream Coat* and played for the school netball team.

Actually sport was a big thing for Phoebe. She tried lots of girly things like ballet and tap dancing, and the violin, but seemed happier when a ball was involved. She loved all things to do with America and really took to basketball, being the only girl on the local boy's basketball team. At the age of 11 she was asked to join the training squad for south of England junior girls.

She didn't get into Tiffin but hey, this was Harry Potter time and Phoebe expressed a desire to go to boarding school thinking it would be like Hogwarts. We were thinking of moving anyway, so found a school just outside of Guildford that offered weekly boarding. At the time it was in the top 25 in the league tables and following the entrance exam they were happy to offer her a place. Also at the time we had the money so, with Phoebe aged 11, we packed our bags and moved to Dorking.

At no time was there any suggestion that Phoebe might be dyslexic.

Actually in hindsight there were clues - although so small that even the great Hercule Poirot may have overlooked them. Before Phoebe ever started primary school she passed an entrance exam for a local independent school called Putney High School and was offered a place. Due to financial circumstances at the time we had to pass on the offer (unheard of amongst West London's chattering classes!).

A few years later she was invited to go back to sit a repeat test for a rare 'occasional place' that had cropped up - to the surprise of both ourselves and the school she failed to get in. Essentially she hadn't moved forward at the rate they expected.

At the time this was nothing to worry about, although with hindsight it's the little things you need to look for. As an aside Phoebe suffers from hay fever and dyslexics often have problems with allergies - another small clue. She also speaks very quickly and, if you were being picky, could be considered to have some speech and language problems.

Like me she had the 'clumsy gene'. Dyslexic's typically have problems with their motor skills. Phoebe was the sort of person who could play a brilliant game of lacrosse, run full tilt for an hour, score three goals and then trip over the minute she came off the pitch. Good fine motor skills, not such good gross ones.

Fast forward to the year before GCSE. By this time Phoebe is getting solid A and B grades in school exams. She is also playing county lacrosse and has played rugby for the county and London and South East. What more could you want from a daughter. How can she be dyslexic - anyway, what's dyslexia in the first place? The word wasn't really in our vocabulary.

Enter Mrs David who points out that Phoebe was a great performer in class and got top marks for her homework, but never achieved the same results in exams. She advised us to get Phoebe tested for dyslexia as she thinks her exam B grades should be A grades, and her A grades should be A*. We know that she has always been a slow reader, and it transpires that she is taking three times as long as her peers to do her 'prep'. She is losing marks in exams by not being able to finish the papers, or rushing and making mistakes.

We call in an Educational Psychologist and sure enough Phoebe is assessed as dyslexic - she has an IQ that puts her in the top 10% of the population, but is underperforming in certain areas. In particular she is not a good reader - she is given a coloured acetate overlay to put over the pages of anything she reads. She is allotted 25% extra time for her GCSEs and duly delivers 6 A* and 4 A grades.

During A level year, by which time Phoebe is now playing lacrosse internationally for Wales, she decided not to pursue her educational career at a UK University, but to go to America. She does her own research, and ends up winning a full scholarship to Johns Hopkins, a top 20 university in America, just outside famous Ivy League schools like Harvard and Princeton. She actually has her place and her scholarship before final A levels, based on American SAT tests. With her foot slightly off the gas she gets 1 As and 2 Bs.

Universities take a more relaxed view of dyslexia - Professors would rather test the depth of your knowledge than the speed at which you can write answers. Now in the US she gets 50% extra time for exams, and is maintaining a GPA (grade point average) of around 3.5 which is equal to a high 2:1 in UK terms.

Phoebe's sporting achievements peaked by playing in the Under 19 Lacrosse World Cup in Canada. This was something of an emotional roller coaster as before every match her self-esteem would really drop and we'd often have tears. Having finished the tournament, playing through the pain barrier of injury, and voted her team's Player of the Tournament', Phoebe admitted that the best part about the entire experience was 'what I've learned about myself'.

I'm not including these achievements in any paternal sense of pride (though that's a given). Rather it's quite amazing to think that it had taken 18 years for this bright and accomplished person to really have belief in herself. I sometimes think dyslexics go through life constantly looking over their shoulder for approval, worrying they'll be 'found out' and endlessly seeking acknowledgement that they are doing it right.

Slightly beset by injury Phoebe has put her sport on hold for the time being although without doubt the high levels of respect her sport gave her was very important in maintaining her self esteem. It doesn't fall to many of us to score goals in a World Cup of any sort. Currently she is carving out something of a career as a sport's staff writer on the college newspaper.

She writes and uses words beautifully although, like me, she has the frustrations of not always finding the right word in time for a conversation. As a family we don't talk specifically about each others challenges much - it's just always there in the background and duly allowed for. However talking to her about this essay she was prompted to send me a poem she wrote at Uni as part of a creative writing course. In many ways it says it all:

The Word Eater
He sits at the tip of your tongue,
licking his lips and waiting,
anticipating, the next big word,
the punch line, the ...
And you're left,
with a thing-a-ma-jig or a
watch-a-ma-call-it?
While he claws at and devours,
That Word.
The one you needed.
Its hours before you finally find it.
After a day of searching it appears
when you no longer want it,
its redundancy rings -
"Malevolent, malevolent!"

Belly full, he laughs, satisfied.

The quite scary truth is that there is every chance Phoebe's dyslexia might never have been picked up. Even so she would probably have been a high achiever, she would just have been among the ranks of undiagnosed adult dyslexics. Now she is definitely aware of her dyslexia and understands in detail the way she has to work best to fulfil her own potential. She has evolved highly developed strategies and exacting time management tactics. And writes poignant poems.

Appendix 2 - the Freddie conundrum

Freddie was a singular child. He was born face presenting and very handsome. He didn't crawl but walked very young. He didn't go through the 'baby-babble' stage of speech, waiting to speak until he was three then speaking in complete sentences. He suffers from eczema and has asthma - again the auto-immune system allergy clue.

Actually from the moment he first went to school Freddie always looked like struggling. He went to the same excellent state primary as Phoebe, but absolutely hated it. One of the very youngest in his year (born mid-July) he wasn't lucky with his teacher - an inexperienced sort who embarrassed him and belittled him in front of the class. On many occasions he cried so much he had to be brought back home. The Head Teacher, a star in most respects, simply didn't accept dyslexia existed having the attitude that whatever the problem 'they'll grow out of it'.

Freddie was singularly failing to perform and was very unhappy - so we bit the bullet and moved him very early on to a local prep school where he spent a year not really getting anywhere but being happier. When Phoebe moved school and we moved house, Freddie moved school again to a different prep school in Cobham. He had been for a 'test day' and we were told that whilst the school would be happy to take him he would need special support from the day he arrived - which firstly came as something of a shock to me as I knew he was a bright boy, then as a relief as I had finally accepted there was a problem.

Freddie was tiny - always one of the shortest and smallest in his year. Early on I had had to tell him how to handle bullies - and on a couple of occasions he had been brave enough to make a pre-emptive strike when being put upon. One episode involved the application of a cricket bat to an adversary's head - luckily the Deputy Head took the view it was deserved self-defence!

Freddie was assessed when Phoebe was assessed. He was already on Special Needs support and the assessment only really confirmed what we all guessed - he was dyslexic. Unusually (according to the Educational Psychologist) he was incredibly similar to Phoebe in terms of IQ and high achieving areas. However his weaknesses were more marked, possibly because Phoebe had received a lot of coaching earlier on and he hadn't, possibly because dyslexia in boys tends to be more severe.

Freddie was a poor reader. He held his pen/pencil in a vice like grip - typical of dyslexics - and struggled to write. His spelling was dreadful. Basically for the first 10 years of his life he was virtually illiterate.

Conversely in speech he was very articulate with a great vocabulary and strong powers of reasoning. Verbally in the classroom his performance was excellent. He had a classic dyslexic profile - he could talk the talk but he couldn't read or write.

He has had to work incredibly hard to catch up and he has had extensive extra one-to-one support. Essentially, learning strategies to compensate for his dyslexia has been a major extra-curricular activity - in effect 'Dyslexia studies' was another whole subject for him. It has been extremely tiring for him, and the concentration required has been awesome. During term-time he forever seemed to have dark rings under his eyes. Typically dyslexics get a lot more tired.

It was very important for him to have chill-time. Some parents limit access to the TV and computer but we simply took the view it was a good way to learn. Freddie has quite sophisticated computer gaming skills. Another hobby was making and painting Warhammer figures and this was something he seemed to resort to when things got tough and he needed a still space in his life. He loved trading card games. As a parent there is always a risk that you become too focused on the school work and keeping-up. Play is important.

My wife points out that unlike Phoebe and myself Freddie's motor skills problems were the other way round. He was great playing with a ball or on monkey bars but couldn't do jigsaws or stuff like Lego. Gluing together Warhammer models and painting the fine detail really helped develop his fine motor skills. (I have to confess that I got into painting Warhammer too, and that the two of us had one brilliant day at a White Dwarf convention at the NEC in Birmingham. Bizarre, but brilliant anyway!)

The turning point academically came when he took RE a year early as a half-GCSE. He actually scored 100% in the exam. Turning the B grades into As across the board a year later was a lot easier because he knew what it took to get an A. Perhaps Freddie's greatest asset academically is knowing how to 'peak' for exams. He reckons sitting at the front in class and learning all he can in the lesson gets him a B, then doing a practice paper or two and revising gently (he's no great reviser) lifts him up a grade.

Revision is left to the last minute. This can be frustrating as a parent but, as he says, he has a typical dyslexic's short term memory and that if he revised earlier he simply wouldn't remember it. He readily understands that a lot of what he learned for GCSE was there to quickly be forgotten. He was bright enough to see that learning was a means to an end. Then again he never wanted to be an expert on Romeo and Juliet.

In terms of self-esteem, just like his sister, sport was his saviour - he was good at football, had played Surrey regional cricket at the age of 11, and was an exciting hockey player. However even sport can be a frustrating area of self-esteem as, if sport is what you are perceived to be good at, but you're not picked for the team, it can be a blow. Being small doesn't help. If you have a child like this be prepared for sensitive management and emergency pizza.

Subsequently Freddie has gone on to play for Wales (at hockey) and at the age of 14 was picked for the Under 16 side, then at 16 for the Under 18 side. He's still one of the smallest boys in the team, and at his college, but even in the testosterone driven years of adolescence being an international athlete gives you good 'street cred' amongst your peer group. It's meant schlepping up and down motorways to Cardiff and Wrexham but, with European and domestic medals round his neck, it's been worth it.

I think the point is here that whether it's painting Warhammer or playing the guitar, or scoring a goal in a house match, singing in the choir or doing lighting for the school play, it's important for dyslexic people to understand what it feels like to achieve. Take a child fishing and it's important they catch a fish first time out - it doesn't matter what size it is, it can be a minnow, it is that sense of success that moves them forward. Once they understand what success looks and feels like they will work out how to get more of it.

Appendix 3 - the me conundrum

Discovering I was dyslexic at the age of 50 came as something of a surprise. You tend not to get that many dyslexic writers, it rather goes against the expectation, although there are some very fine ones. Words and language are my stock in trade and I've made a living using them, predominantly in written format.

Indeed I learned my alphabet before I went to school, and I could tell the time and recite the days of the week and months of the year very early on. My father, who left school at the age of 14 and joined the forces, was a great believer in education, and helped me learn to read and write. I was naturally inquisitive, and learned heaps from my mother and my Grandmother who was a country-woman who had chickens in her garden and used to take me for walks in the woods and tell me stuff.

With hindsight I may have been a bit of a precocious pain at my primary school which was pretty new and built to accommodate a burgeoning population in the London overspill town in which we lived. We were taught by rote by some quite ferocious teachers, most of whom we viewed with fear rather than respect - hey, that was the due order of things back in the day.

There was heaps of repetition, loads of practice writing and spelling, and a real focus on reading, writing and arithmetic for the very sake of it. We didn't do a lot of topic based work, when we were doing spelling we were doing spelling so we sat still and we recited our spellings over and over. We were allowed the time to do stuff, and in those days in those places there was very little extra-curricular activity to distract us.

We also learned great listening skills from the radio. There was not much television - either a TV or the programming - so we used to sit in enraptured silence to Listen with Mother. I also remember very clearly listening to boxing on the radio with my Grandparents - quite a bizarre concept these days but I still love to hear a good fight sitting staring into the middle distance visualising the blow by blow action.

People used to read out loud to us, and reading, when it's all the entertainment you've got, becomes very aspirational. The best day of the week was always comic day. Nearly everybody had a comic and those that didn't would be offered a share. Seeing all those words in speech balloons in close context with drawings made reading so much easier.

I passed the 11 plus and went to Grammar school where my parents were quite amazed I think to be told at an early parents' day that I would get to university. Nobody from my family, my street, my council estate or even my area of town had gone to Uni to the best of my knowledge. Scary!

In those days we took O levels and I duly passed English and Maths in the fourth form and then sat 10 more in the fifth form. Here I failed Latin and Additional Maths - Latin because I couldn't get my head round it and Additional Maths because a) I couldn't see the point of knowing how to work out the height of a telegraph pole and b) by the fifth form I was playing sport in all the senior teams and classes clashed with match days. I knew my priorities!

In the sixth form I took three A levels and got B, B, and C grades - sufficient to get me offers at every Uni I wanted to get to with the exception of Cambridge where I had been encouraged to apply by the Headmaster. I used to hang out with the crowd in the Art Room and was persuaded to do another O level in Art, was House Captain, sang in the choir, was on the debating team, and roadie for the school rock band. I ended up at University College London.

It all sounds pretty good but the point is I wasn't unusual. There were better boys than me at everything, better sportsmen, boys with more O and A levels at better grades. I was just seen as a good all rounder. Certainly nobody thought I had special needs. Although, I sometimes wonder what those grades might have been had I been recognised as dyslexic and given the attention on offer today.

Looking back the clues were there. I have always had a disastrous memory and would forget to take stuff to school, often on pain of a slapped wrist or posterior. There were certain things I simply couldn't grasp - like the stuff in physics where you use your fingers and thumb to work out which way a current runs round a magnet or something. Or the way to work out the volume of a cone (hey, see how much ice-cream you can get in it!)

In those days written exams were often 3 hours long - and we couldn't take in drinks or a snack so no wonder so many of us came out with a headache. Even so I often couldn't finish the papers. The only exam/study skill I was taught was to get the easy points first and hope to get through to the end. With hindsight, I needed extra time, but the old fashioned view was that time pressure was part of performance.

Latin was difficult but French was fine. I put this down to my Dad teaching me to listen to the music. I have always had a good ear and recognise accents very easily. Latin not being a spoken language I couldn't make sense of it. I did have major speech and language problems in the form of a mind-bogglingly embarrassing stammer.

I was also very bad at reading out loud - something that, since talking to other adult dyslexics about this book, I discover is very common. It seems to be that in between reading something on a page and translating it to speech, we either forget what the words were, or they change. Likewise I was never any good at acting because for the life of me I couldn't remember the lines. These days there are any number of great movie actors who are dyslexic, but very few on the stage. The 'short takes' structure of film makes remembering lines much more straightforward.

To get over this I joined the debating team but well up into my thirties my most frustrating and embarrassing moments would occur when I knew the answer, or had a smart comment, but couldn't speak when I wanted to, and then someone else spoke up and the moment had passed. In my early advertising career some people used to affectionately call me 'Stutts' - well they thought it was affectionate.

I was not much good at remembering formulae either. How I passed Chemistry A level is still a mystery shrouded in mystery. We were the very first year A level year to do multiple choice questions, we were the experiment. All I can think of is that the examining board cocked it up so badly they gave everybody a C grade in commiseration.

I wanted to do English but was pushed into being a scientist. I was told that I wrote fairly amusing stories but that the Head of English didn't really see me handling the classics of English Literature. I realise now that I worked out my own strategies for compensating for the poor memory. I used to write everything down - the very act of writing got it into my brain better. Come revision time I would make notes of my notes until I got down to a single one word prompt. Words have been my saviour.

I also have the auto-immune allergy clue. All my childhood I had a chronic sniff and now in later life I have developed serious hayfever. Even today on occasion I still stutter. Even now my memory is not good and I realise I have developed a litany of sub-vocalised strategies (that is to say I talk to myself!) to remember my keys, my phone, my watch, my money etc, etc. Had I ever got to Cambridge I would by now without doubt be an 'absent minded Professor'!

Did it matter at the time? Not really at all I don't think. When I came out of Uni (with a third Class Honours in Geography) in the mid 70's the miner's strike was just finished, interest rates were at 15% and they'd cut back on Graduate Training. Luckily there were very few graduates around so I went into a variety of sales roles, invariably following an interview where they couldn't believe such a 'highly qualified' person wanted that sort of job, then into marketing and advertising.

The beauty about being a copy writer is that all you need to do is write a few compelling lines, preferably with a joke at the end. Keep on making them laugh or cry and you stay in work. Then I started to get into strategic thinking, business analysis and all those other problem solving areas at which dyslexics excel.

The marketing business, with its core values of competition, and reward for innovation that leads to success, is a great industry if you have a creative problem-solving mind that works like mine. Thanks to being dyslexic I have never had 'writers block' as I see things different ways, or many ways at once. I never have to search for ideas, they are just always there. Just like this essay, which I didn't really plan at all, it just came out in this order.

There must be thousands of undiagnosed dyslexics my age like me, taught by rote and pushed through a regimented and rigorous system that quite suited our learning requirements. Most of them I should think happily and blissfully unaware that they have a condition that qualifies them as 'Disabled'.

Appendix 4 - the non-dyslexic Mummy conundrum

Given the genetic conundrum that dyslexia seems to pass more readily down the male line, and the fact that assessing for dyslexia has only become common in the last few years, there are heaps of non-diagnosed dyslexic men in the real world. The majority of them will have non-dyslexic partners. I'm not sure if it works the other way round, but on the basis that opposites attract there's a good chance.

I don't remember if I was ever really concerned about the children's dyslexia until something had to be done about it - in which case we did something about it. The dyslexic male may be unaware or blithe but once there is a problem to solve he is rarely indecisive. However it meant that the bulk of the pressure fell upon my wife.

She saw the frustration and the tears close-up and personal. She saw the other children in the playground. She talked to the teachers. In an increasingly competitive world she also faced the peer group pressure. Of course being non-dyslexic, and with dyslexia at the time being something of an unfashionable condition with connotations of dimness, she had enormous frustrations of her own.

In my experience Mummies intuitively know the potential of their children and manage them accordingly. In Freddie's case in particular my wife's views were diametrically opposed to both the apparent reality and the school perspective - ultimately she was totally justified in believing she knew them best.

I always think that if ever my wife came back to earth as a dog she'd be a terrier. When the obvious became inevitable she discovered all she could about dyslexia, got a job as a classroom assistant and got herself on a range of courses until now she rejoices in more letters after her name than Lord Mandelson. In terms of her qualifications the correct mode of address now appears to be Mrs Fleur Campbell, B.A. (Hons) OCR Dip (SpLD), SpLD APC (Patoss) No. 500001041-5015.

Her day job is to teach the next generation of teachers who specialise in Specific Learning Disorders (hence SpLD), and assess young and old alike to see if they are dyslexic. In assessing younger children she always gets the chance to talk to Mummies who are going through all the uncertainties and worries she went through. Increasingly she sees Daddies too, many of whom, when told about the problems their child is facing, come to the realisation they may well be dyslexic themselves.

About the author

Al Campbell didn't discover he was dyslexic until he was 50. By then both his children had been assessed as dyslexic, and his wife Fleur had become so interested in the subject that she had gone to college and studied for 5 years to become a dyslexia specialist and assessor. Having spent the majority of his life making a living as a writer and copywriter, the discovery came as something of a surprise.

Al hails from a small town in Kent where he went to a state primary school on the council estate on which he was born, before attending the local Grammar school. He ended up at University College London where he scraped a poor degree in Geography but took first class honours in poker. He graduated just after the miner's strike when interest rates were 15% and graduate jobs were hard to come by. Unable to secure a hoped-for job in a big London agency he went into sales and eventually started his own advertising business.

He has always written. He started with school plays and magazine articles when he was younger, first made money from his pen by writing short stories for men's magazines, and then, in advertising, worked as a copywriter on brands as diverse as British Aerospace, Club 18-30, Pricewaterhouse Coopers, ABN Amro and many others.

In more recent years Al has become a strategic business planner and consultant, something he finds comes easily to what he now knows to be his dyslexic brain: ' dyslexics are natural problem solvers,' he says, 'we have to be because most of us can't remember how we did something from one time to the next so we keep reinventing stuff and trying it different ways.'

Al, who is now 56, lives in Sussex with his wife, his son Freddie, and his two springers Holly and Ruby. His daughter Phoebe is currently studying at Johns Hopkins University in Baltimore USA.

To contact Al email: adyslexicwrites@hotmail.co.uk